MW00939862

Deer Stand
Revelations

Deer Stand Revelations

MARTY R. PERKINS

XULON PRESS

Xulon Press
2301 Lucien Way #415
Maitland, FL 32751
407.339.4217
www.xulonpress.com

© 2021 by Marty R. Perkins

All rights reserved solely by the author. The author
guarantees all contents are original and do not
infringe upon the legal rights of any other person or
work. No part of this book may be reproduced in any
form without the permission of the author. The views
expressed in this book are not necessarily those of
the publisher.

Due to the changing nature of the Internet, if there
are any web addresses, links, or URLs included in
this manuscript, these may have been altered and
may no longer be accessible. The views and opinions
shared in this book belong solely to the author and
do not necessarily reflect those of the publisher. The
publisher therefore disclaims responsibility for the
views or opinions expressed within the work.

Unless otherwise indicated, Scripture quotations taken
from the New King James Version (NKJV). Copyright
© 1982 by Thomas Nelson, Inc. Used by permission.
All rights reserved.

Printed in the United States of America.

Paperback ISBN-13: 978-1-6628-1531-7
eBook ISBN-13: 978-1-6628-1532-4

FIRST GLIMPSE

I have always had a love for the outdoors. From hunting and fishing to working and playing; I have spent most of my life outside. When God saved me, I went from loving the outdoors to having a passion for His creation. God began to speak to me and reveal Himself to me when I was in the deer stand or when I was walking through the woods or standing beside a body of water with a fishing pole in my hand. God showed me purpose in His wonderful creation and taught me lessons through success and failure in my hunting and fishing adventures. He sent me back to my childhood and gave meaning to the good and bad things that I had seen and lived. He blessed me with understanding in the cruel things that have transpired and are transpiring in a lost world. Through a gentle whisper in the wind or a beautiful note from a songbird, He gave me hope. Through a misplaced arrow or errant shot, He brought back memories of things that special people in my life had said many years ago. In my successes afield, He gave me provision and taught me to be thankful.

God did not give me all these revelations to keep within myself. He clearly showed me through His Word and His constant urging (conviction), that He had given me these stories, life events and understanding in them, so that I would share them with others. It took me many years to answer His call to write it all down to share with the world or the few who would read it. If only one person reads it and is somehow changed or touched by it; it has all been worth it. I sincerely hope and pray that each person who reads it gains a little better appreciation for God's amazing creation and more importantly, a better understanding of our Lord and who He really is.

In all cases, whenever I reference God as Him or He, I will capitalize. For the glory is all His. I refuse to capitalize satan and give him any credit.

Marty Perkins

SOMEONE HAD TO DIE

Years ago, I had a friend who had received a liver transplant. After his recovery, I overheard someone tell him one day that they were happy for him. He responded by saying, "I'm happy and thankful also but I can never lose sight of the fact that somebody had to die in order for me to live." I've never forgotten my friend Ronnie's words that day.

That memory comes back to me every time I'm hunting and I'm fortunate enough to kill an animal. I respect the fact that in order for me to live (eat), animals must die. I'm thankful, a little sad, and tremendously humble each time.

My Savior, Jesus Christ, had to die so that you and I may live. I pray that I never lose sight of that and I remain humble and thankful for it.

2 Corinthians 5:21

❧ 2 ❧

A TRUE CALLING

I t was the first day of turkey season and an absolutely beautiful April morning; I was sitting at the base of a huge oak tree waiting for the morning light to appear. Hoping to hear a big ole Tom turkey gobble, I was filled with excitement and anticipation. I had heard a gobbler fly up to roost the previous evening and let out a thunderous gobble to let all his hens know where he was and that he would be ready for breeding in the morning.

As dawn began to come alive, I was about to make a few soft yelps and clucks to see if I could get that ole gobbler stirred up. Before I could make a call however, a real hen started yelping. At least, I thought it was a real hen. As I listened closely, I began to wonder if I was hearing the real thing or whether there was another hunter on the adjoining property. I quickly realized that the other call was another hunter and I slipped out of there in the opposite direction. No turkey is worth getting shot over.

How did I recognize the yelps as being another hunter instead of a real hen? First of all, the calling was too loud. Tree yelps from a real hen are normally very soft and subtle. Secondly, the calling was almost too perfect. Anyone who has ever heard a real hen turkey knows that they usually sound horrible, raspy, and anything but perfect.

A call from God is sometimes difficult to recognize as being real. We need to be able to determine authentic calls from God versus callings from ourselves. How do we do that? What I have found in my own life is that a true calling from God is usually not comfortable and it requires me to get out of my comfort zone. Rarely does God call me to do something that I feel like I am prepared for, equipped for, or good at. A true calling from God will seldom make sense to the world. Answering God's call, for me, has meant pushing forward over every barrier and obstacle and saying, "okay, Lord, I'll put me aside and trust You." Here are some things that Jesus never says to anyone when He is placing a call on their life:

(1) Let's evaluate your strengths, your talents, your gifts.
(2) First, let's look at how well you do certain things.
(3) Let's look at what you're comfortable with.
(4) Let's see what resources you have.

Jesus did say in Matthew 4:19, "Follow Me, and I will make you fishers of men." I have found that the only requirements for me are to trust Him—trust Him to supply everything needed, trust Him to change the call at any time while I'm answering the call—and to take up my cross and follow Him. By taking up my cross, I am deciding to put myself and my needs and desires to the side. Taking up my cross, and not dying on it (dying to self), is at best a courageous attempt at being selfish.

I'd like to share one of the greatest callings I've ever had in my life. It began sometime in late 2015 or early 2016. It started when I saw, over and over on social media, that a lady I didn't even know, named Donna Wilborn, needed a kidney due to kidney disease. At first, I was touched by her story, but that's as far as it went. Then, as I saw more and more about her and her situation, I began to pray for her. It seemed that every time I went on social media, I saw more and more about her and her dire need for a kidney donor. I became increasingly burdened by her situation and began praying daily for her and that she would find a donor.

I remember one night waking up in the very early hours of the morning and vividly seeing her face in my mind. I began praying. The burden became almost unbearable. I couldn't believe what I started thinking. There was no way that God could be calling me to donate a kidney to this lady who I didn't even know, *could He?* For weeks I struggled with what seemed to be a real calling. One minute, my mind and heart said *"yes,*

Lord." The next minute my mind and heart were saying "*no way, are you crazy?*" or "*this is ridiculous.*" I kept this within me and didn't tell anyone for fear that they would think that I surely was crazy. This went on for weeks. I didn't sleep well during that time and I was broken and burdened. That's when I started realizing that it truly was a call from God.

Then came the day of reckoning. At about the same time all of this was going on, we found out that our son-in-law's father, Andy Strader, also needed a kidney. If he didn't get a donor soon, he would have to go on dialysis. Of course, my wife and I were praying for him. I wish I knew the exact date, but I can't recall. I was about to head out of the door to go to work. I went upstairs like I always did to tell my wife Johnsie goodbye and give her a kiss. I could tell something was on her mind and I asked her what was wrong. She just hesitated and looked at me. My first inclination was to think that I had done something or said something to upset her. That surely has happened a time or two in our marriage. Then she began to speak hesitantly. I'll never forget exactly what she said. She said, "would you think I have gone crazy if I said that I feel like I have been called to give Andy a kidney?" I immediately had so many emotions. A mixture of surprise, shock, relief, and unbelievable understanding and love for my amazing wife consumed me. I really don't think she expected the reply I gave her. I recall it so well. I said, "no, I don't think you're crazy at all."

"Would you think I was crazy if I told you that I have the same calling for Donna Wilborn?" There was complete silence for what seemed like forever. Then we both burst into tears as we hugged one another. We both went to work that day with a lot on our minds.

We both came home that night from work wondering what we were going to do and how we would proceed with this calling. I didn't know what to do, so I contacted Donna and told her that I wanted to try to be a donor for her and asked what I needed to do to get started. She gave me the phone number and told me who I needed to talk to at Duke. At the time, we didn't tell anyone else about this, and Johnsie didn't say anything to Andy about her intentions.

We got in touch with the Duke transplant team and had our first appointments. We had to go to information sessions, have complete health physicals and numerous tests, including psychological examinations. We both seemed to be good donor candidates. Now it was a matter of whether we were good matches for our intended recipients. During one appointment, I remember both of us talking to one of the surgeons at the same time. He told us that we would be making history by being the first couple at Duke to be kidney donors at the same time. I believe that the surgeon's positivity was the beginning of the huge letdown that was about to come for me.

A few weeks later, Johnsie received a call from Duke saying that she was a perfect match for Andy and that they needed for her to come in and sign some documents and set a date for the surgery. We went to that appointment and the date was set. Of course, Andy would have to agree to the date and go through some health tests before it was finalized. At the time, we had not told anyone about this, so we had to set up a meeting with Andy and his family and our family to tell them. When we arrived at Andy's house, they all were thinking that we had set up a surprise vacation or trip of some sort. They were shocked, to say the least when Johnsie announced that on August 29, 2016, she would be donating her kidney to Andy. Wow, that was an amazing time of rejoicing, hugging, and answered prayer.

In the meantime, I received a call from Duke while at work one day telling me that I wasn't a match for Donna but that there was still an option. They told me about a program called shared donor in which Donna and I could be matched with another donor and recipient that matched us. My kidney would go to the matched recipient and Donna would receive a kidney from the matched donor. They said that this actually is more common than you would think. So, I was a little disheartened but still had hope. I shared this news with Donna and told her that this wasn't over yet. I had to go for even more tests at Duke and everything was going well.

Then came the day that Johnsie and I had to talk to the surgeons who would be performing the transplant operations on her and Andy. They also wanted to take my blood pressure and do a few more blood tests on me. A few days later, I received a call from Duke that crushed me. They told me that I was not going to be able to be a donor because of my blood pressure. My blood pressure was on the high end of normal range, but they said that it was too risky because when you donate a kidney, your blood pressure automatically elevates and that it was not a good idea for me to donate. I was still willing, but Duke was not. That left me with the chore of contacting Donna to tell her that I couldn't be her donor. I felt like I had let her down so badly; that was one of the lowest points of my life.

I began questioning God and questioning the call. I was so sure that He had called me to this. The call was uncomfortable and not of this world, so I believed with everything in me that this call was from Him and that it was real. I was completely confused, upset, sad, and mad. I actually felt betrayed by God, and my faith took a major hit. I forgot that God promised to always be with me and to give me exactly what I need and that His callings are perfect. In the days ahead, it seemed as if I was in a fog. At Johnsie's final appointment at Duke before the transplant surgery, one of the psychiatrists talked to both of us separately and asked so many questions. One of the questions she asked me was how I felt about the possibility of something going wrong during the transplant surgery and how I felt about Johnsie's decision to do this. I think my answer threw her off guard. I told her that I knew that this was a calling from God for Johnsie and that I was prepared for whatever God's plan was in it. I told her that I understood because I had answered what I thought was the same call. That's when it hit me. God did call me to go through all that I went through to try and be a donor for Donna. It was a real call from Him. I realized at that moment that God had called me to this so that I would understand Johnsie's call. Without my call, I never would have understood her call and I would have fought it tooth and nail. God knew exactly what He needed to put me through in order for Johnsie's perfect call to come to fruition. Accepting God's will in one's own life is one matter. Accepting God's will in the lives of those you love the most is something altogether different.

When God calls you to something and you are obedient, He will make a way. Sometimes, a thimble full of obedience translates into a truck load of fruit. The transplant surgery was successful, and Andy and Johnsie are doing great. All of the negative things that are supposed to happen to a kidney donor never happened to Johnsie. I guess God didn't read the post-surgery problem list. Her blood pressure is lower than before surgery and her kidney function levels in her remaining kidney are perfect. Donna received a kidney from a wonderful donor who answered her calling, and they both are doing great also. By the way, that ole gobbler in the first part of this story succumbed to my shotgun the following morning. The other hunter had to go back to work. God is good.

Romans 8:28; 1 Corinthians 7:17.

⚜ 3 ⚜

WEATHERING THE STORM

I t was the middle of the night and March was making its approach like a roaring lion. A major cold front had brought a rain, sleet, and snow mixture all day on February 28. The ground was saturated. It was a real mess. The howling wind was gusting at 50–60 mph, and I was thankful to have a roof over my head and a warm bed to sleep in. But sleep didn't come easy as I was concerned about the combination of a saturated ground and strong winds toppling trees. It sounded as if it was going to blow our log home down. We lost power sometime in the early morning hours. I was mentally prepared for the worst come sunrise.

As a new dawn approached on March 1, I began to peek outside to see the expected destruction. To my surprise, all the trees seemed to be standing. There was debris, leaves, and limbs laying everywhere but no trees were down. I checked with my son's and daughter's families and they were all good and didn't have any trees down either. I went outside and began surveying our property. I checked the trees that I normally have tree stands in. I was completely shocked that I couldn't find a tree down anywhere.

I began to wonder how all the trees survived the storm. The only thing I could attribute it to was that the winds of the past had made the roots on the trees strong over the years, giving them a good foundation. Every breeze and every storm had tested the root systems, challenged them, and made them stronger. I guess you could say that they had stood up to the test.

In our lives, we must endure things that would be too difficult for us to handle without our winds of the past. God knows exactly what storms we will face and how strong the "gusts" will be every day for the rest of our lives. He also knows exactly what we need to go through in order to strengthen us for what is to come. So, when our lives are windy, will we blow over or will we lean on Jesus and let Him strengthen our foundation? We should always search for the positive in all things that life throws at us. That's not an easy task, but it's doable when we understand that God has either brought the storm to us or is allowing us to be in it for our good. Below are the lyrics to a song that God gave me several years ago when a storm was approaching.

Which Way Will I Go?

When the storms of life come crashing down around me,
Will I run to You or will I turn away?
Will I pray and let Your loving grace surround me?
Will I fall or will I seek Your face?
Will I take the road less traveled or will I take the beaten path?
Will I come unraveled or will I stay composed?
Lord, tell me, which way will I go?

When I'm faced with things that happen
That I don't understand,
Will I remember all Your promises to me?
Will I reach out and let You take me by the hand?
Will I submit and get down on my knees?
Will I say that I can't handle this, I give it all to You?
Will I lean on You or face it all alone?
Lord tell me, which way will I go?

Which way will I go?
It's something that I really need to know.
Lord, tell me, which way will I go?

When I'm dealing with adversity because I follow You
Will I control my anger, or will I succumb?
Will I say and do some things I know I shouldn't do?
Will I revert to hate or handle it with love?
Will I argue with uncertainty or witness with Your word?
Will I back off or share the things I know?

Lord, tell me, which way will I go?

Which way will I go?
It's something that I really need to know.
Lord, tell me, which way will I go?

James 1:2–5; Psalm 9:9–10; Job 38:1–6.

⚜ 4 ⚜

LIVING ON THE EDGE

E very year it's the same. Every year I do the same things. On our 65-acre property, I plant food plots each spring. Most years, I have planted clover of some variety. After turkey season, I begin to supplement feed the deer herd and other wildlife with corn. I set up trail cameras in order to watch the antler growth of the current year's buck crop and to generally see what kind of wildlife is showing up to feed. Every year, I have many bucks, does, and fawns and there are usually a couple of nice shooter bucks that I watch all summer in hopes of having an opportunity to harvest them when bow season arrives in the fall.

Some years, I have been successful and have taken a few nice bucks during the first couple of weeks of bow season. Some years, I haven't been successful at all; then it happens, sometimes before bow season and sometimes a couple weeks into bow season. The acorns begin to fall off the trees and all of my bucks seem to disappear. It's like overnight magic; the deer aren't eating the corn or the clover and I'm not getting any pictures on my trail cameras of any nice bucks. I make all sorts of excuses as to why the bucks are no longer showing themselves. That the neighbors have better food plots is one that always enters my mind. Farmers on all sides of my property have larger fields than I do and usually plant either corn or soybeans. Another one is that somebody has illegally shot the big bucks at night or legally with depredation permits. I've also used the excuse that coyotes or stray dogs have run them all off. I have come up with every excuse to avoid the truth.

The truth is that the acorns are falling. That's it. That's all. Acorns are a whitetail's favorite food source, and they will abandon all other food sources to feed on them. It's kind of like a child that has a choice of candy or meatloaf. They like meatloaf but certainly not as much as candy. Most of my property was timbered a few years back and there are very few large oak trees that are old enough to produce acorns. However, there are a few in the center of my property in the bottom near the creek. So, there's a simple solution for all of this, right? I can just go set up stands near those oaks and all my big bucks will be there, right?

It's just not that simple, at least not for me. I have always hunted the outer edges or outer perimeter of my property. For one thing, that's where my food plots are and also hunting the outer edges requires less effort. It's easier to put up deer stands and it's easier to supplement feed and put out mineral sites/attractants. But those are not the main reasons that I don't venture beyond the edges of my property. The real reason is that I have a fear of going into the core of my property during hunting season for any reason. I fear that I will spook the deer out of their bedding area or leave too much scent. I'm afraid to take the chance of running the bigger bucks off of my property for good. It seems as if I've always been content to either be unsuccessful or, at best, shoot mediocre bucks. As of today, the beginning of the second week of bow season 2020, I have not overcome that fear completely. The acorns are falling, my bucks have disappeared, and I know what I need to do. I'm searching for the courage to do what I know I need to do.

I believe that, as Christians, we face some of those same fears. Most Christians, including me, spend most of their Christian walk on the outer edges of their faith. For instance, we sometimes seem to dwell in a few chosen verses of Scripture from God's Word. John 3:16, the golden rule, love thy neighbor, judge not, and a few others are where many Christians remain for most of their Christian lives. Those verses are all good as is all of God's Word. However, God has much more to say to us if we would have the courage to venture into the deepest corners of His Word. Perhaps we are afraid of what we will find if we take in all of God's Word. Perhaps there will be something there uncomfortable for us. Perhaps there will be revelation from Him or a calling that we don't want to be obedient to. Perhaps life is good just being saved by His grace and we don't want to upset our Utopia.

The truth is that most of us as Christians never enjoy the bounty and the blessings that God desires for us because we live in fear. We seem to be content with our fire insurance as I call it. We give very little thought to being about the works that God created us for. We rarely or never lead anyone to Christ because we just live on the outer perimeter of what God has appointed us to and called us to. We all were created by God, in His image, for special purposes and actions. Rarely do we discover all of the purposes He has created us for, and seldom do we fulfill all of the deeds He desires for us to accomplish because we are afraid.

God has called us to be bold and courageous in our faith. We are living in troubled times in our world today and we can point fingers in all kinds of directions as to why. Perhaps we need to look at our lack of courage and unwillingness to follow the toughest, innermost parts of what God has commanded us as being the largest contributor to our troubles.

In revealing this to me, God has laid it on my heart that I need to dig deeper into His Word, ask for revelation from it, and apply it to my daily walk. I've got to go move a deer stand.

> 2 Timothy 3:16; Joshua 1:9.

⚔ 5 ⚔

LIVING WATER

There is a small creek that runs through the center of our property. I often go there to sit and study God's Word or to build a small fire and just reflect on life and pray. There is a freshwater spring that feeds the creek that comes in behind our pond dam. When the weather is dry, the water from the spring to the creek tends not to flow and it becomes stagnant. In dry times, there are very few deer tracks where the stagnant water is. It seems as if the deer would rather drink from the moving or "living" water as I like to call it.

I am reminded of a day when one of my grandchildren and I went into a convenience store to grab some lunch. We ordered our lunch from the grill and proceeded to get something from the coolers in the back of the store to drink. As a matter of habit, I went to the cooler that had bottled water in it and my grandchild went to the sugared poison section. I began to look at all of the bright colored concoctions that were meant to attract kids. There was the red tootie fruity poison, the green and blue liquid garbage, and every other color of chemical carbonated artificial flavors. All of them were loaded with sugar and had up to 300–400 calories per bottle. Though I wish I could, there is nothing that I can do about these things being available, but as a grandparent I can say no and as an adult, I can be disciplined enough to refrain from drinking this junk.

I began to think that in life, we have a choice of living water (Jesus) or the sugared waters of the world. Just like the pretty colors of drinks, the world entices us with pretty packages, pretty people, and colorful things. We, as Christians, have the option to be disciplined and refrain or to partake of the sugared waters of this world. We also have the option, as God's creation, to choose living water and never be thirsty again or to be thirsty forever. And as parents and grandparents, kids really do need for us to say no to them and to be able to see us live "no" by example.

John 4:13–15.

6

HOW DO I LOOK?

The last thing I do before I head to my tree stand, especially during bow season is to paint my face with camouflage makeup. The particular brand that I use has a small mirror that allows you to see what you look like once you're done. I usually either use that mirror or look at my reflection in the glass pane on my back door. One day, I was looking at myself after I applied the makeup and it hit me that it really didn't matter what I thought I looked like. What really mattered is what I looked like to the deer. How would they see me? Would they be able to pick me out as a human or would I appear to them as part of a tree or foliage?

When I look into my own bathroom mirror prior to going somewhere, everything can seem to be in place, at least as well as can be expected for me. Then, when I look in the mirror on my wife's car, on the way to church especially, I tend to see all sorts of things that need to be groomed, snatched, plucked, trimmed, or smoothed over. One day, as I was looking into the rearview mirror of my wife's car, I was reminded that in my spiritual walk, I need to be looking at myself through other people's mirrors more so than my own. It is important how others view me; see me. My reflection should be Jesus in my mirror and others' mirrors. My prayer is that I will never become a stumbling block for anyone else.

We, as Christians, need to go to the mirror often to examine ourselves, to look in the mirror, not in vanity but in humility. Look often, walk away, then look again. If you're good looking, I guess it's okay to look a third time. I wouldn't know about that.

1 Samuel 16:7; Romans 14:13.

❧ 7 ❧

WHEN LITTLE IS BIG

I t was mid-September 1984. I was twenty-three years old and didn't have the sense God gave a billy goat. It was my prime time and I thought I was invincible. I had just purchased a two-year-old treeing walker coonhound. I wanted to try him out and see if he was worth the money I had just spent on him. There was a cornfield about a mile from my house where I had permission to hunt. I knew that there would be several bandits trying to steal the neighbor's corn. It would be the perfect place to see what this hound was made of.

As soon as it got dark, I loaded Bad Bob (the coonhound) into my old truck and headed down the road. Yes, I was by myself. My young bride and nine-month-old daughter, Anna, weren't interested in going with me. I arrived at the cornfield and turned Bad Bob out. I had seen a deer standing in the corn when I pulled up and I thought that this would be a good test to see if ole Bad Bob was going to run a deer.

In just a few seconds I heard Bad Bob strike—that means that he barked for you non coon hunters. I immediately thought to myself that he was running that deer. In a couple of minutes however, I heard his bark change and recognized that he was treeing something. As we coon hunters say, "he was blowing the top out of that tree." I turned my light on and walked down to the tree where he was. When I shone my light up the tree, I saw eyes and then was able to make out the silhouette of a very large raccoon.

Coon season was not yet in, so I didn't have a rifle with me. I wanted ole Bad Bob to know that he had done a good job and wanted him to see this coon, so I got the brilliant idea that I would climb the tree and knock that ole coon out to him. Did I mention earlier that I was young, dumb, and invincible? The tree was a huge poplar and was fairly easy to climb. Holding the light with my teeth, I began to climb. Ole Bad Bob was going crazy. I climbed and I climbed until I got very close to the raccoon. All of a sudden, the coon jumped toward me. I should have expected that, don't you think? I was startled and stepped back on the limb I was standing on. I found out very quickly why these trees are named poplar when the limb popped, and I came crashing down.

What happened then is somewhat of a blur. I knew I had fallen and hit several limbs on the way down and that I was in pain. When I hit the ground, ole Bad Bob, thinking I was the biggest coon he had ever seen, sailed on me and sunk his teeth into my coveralls shredding them. In my shock, I smacked him in the head to get him off me. I think he realized then that I wasn't your average coon falling out of a tree. Ole Bad Bob never did tree another coon after that. I guess he thought that I was punishing him and that he had done wrong. I was dazed, hurting, and in shock over what had just happened.

I got back to my truck and drove home in severe pain. I told my wife what had happened, and we began to survey my injuries. I knew I had at least one broken rib, so I had her wrap my mid-section up tightly with a bandage. I had a bad gash in my back from the sharp edge of the broken limb that cut me on my way to the ground. My back was hurting. I found out later that I had a fractured vertebra. My feet hurt from the landing. My arm was bleeding from Bad Bob's teeth, and I had bruises all over.

The following morning, I got up to go to work. Did I mention that I was young, dumb, and invincible? The power plant where I worked was in a shutdown and my daddy was working there also as a contractor. He was riding to work with me every day. I went to pick him up and told him what had happened the night before. The cornfield where all of this took place was on our way to work so I stopped to look at the tree I fell out of and to try and determine how far I fell. When we looked up at the broken limb and how far it was up that tree, my daddy almost had a heart attack. Then we looked on the ground where I had fallen. There were jagged rocks sticking up from the ground all around the tree and I had fallen in between two of them. I went back a few months later and measured the distance from the limb to the ground. It was a few inches shy of forty feet We thanked God, even though I didn't know Him yet, for protecting me. We realized that I could have very easily been killed. Then we proceeded on to work. That was a tough day.

Fast-forward to June 2014. I had just finished mowing with my zero-turn mower and was putting it back into my storage building. My storage building entrance is about three feet off the ground so I had a set of ramps that I used whenever loading or unloading the mower. I got off the mower and proceeded to walk down one of the ramps. Somehow, my foot got caught up in the ramp and I tripped and fell to the ground. Remember, this was from only three feet off the ground.

When I landed, I immediately knew that something was wrong. My left foot, ankle, and left knee were all hurting. The ankle was hurting so bad that I almost passed out. I crawled from my shed back to the house and somehow made it inside. Nurse Johnsie, my wife, went to work on me once again. She wrapped my knee and ankle, got me some ice and some pillows, and I sat in my recliner with both my legs elevated. This was on a Saturday. By Sunday, I couldn't walk without crutches.

On Monday, I went to the doctor who made me an appointment with an orthopedic clinic. I went to the orthopedic doctor on Tuesday. This was two days out of work already. After numerous tests, the prognosis was that I had a broken bone in my left foot, a torn ligament in my left ankle, and torn cartilage in my left knee. I had already had two surgeries on my left knee, a torn ACL, and a torn cartilage from sports injuries. The doctor fitted me with an orthopedic boot for my foot and ankle injuries. He said that in time, they should heal without surgery. He also scheduled a knee surgery to repair the torn cartilage.

The surgery was scheduled for two weeks later, so now I had missed over two weeks of work. I went into surgery thinking that when I woke up everything would be repaired and I could begin the recovery process and get back to work soon. I wasn't prepared for what the orthopedic surgeon told me. He said that after he removed all the damaged cartilage in my knee, there was none left. He said that basically my knee was worn out and that it was bone on bone. He told me that my knee needed to be replaced. He said I didn't have to replace it but that I wouldn't be able to participate in any sports activities or walk without pain. At fifty-two years old, I was still very active and wanted to remain that way for hopefully a long time, so I decided to have my knee replaced. I didn't realize at the time that it just wasn't that simple.

Before the replacement could be scheduled, I had to basically heal from the surgery that I just had. That required physical therapy and rest. While I was recovering, I had to work with the orthopedic doctor to help justify the knee replacement to my insurance company. It was a major headache to say the least. The insurance company required that I try all other alternatives first before they would approve the knee replacement. The physical therapy was the first thing, then they required that I have rooster comb injections, using a ten-inch long needle or so it seemed. During all of these ridiculous attempts at bypassing the replacement, I was out of work. Not only that, but I was unable to bow hunt. After four and a half months of trial and error—and I emphasize error—my insurance company finally approved the knee replacement.

On December 10, I finally had the knee replacement. There is so much I could say about the recovery process but that is another story. The bottom line is that six weeks after the knee replacement, I was back at work. If the insurance company had approved the replacement in June, I would have only missed about eight weeks of work total. As it was, however, I had missed six months of work.

The point of comparing these two life events is that sometimes a little thing (falling three feet), can have a greater impact than something that we would consider a major thing (falling forty feet). A small gesture of kindness or a little encouragement can have huge implications in people's lives. Sometimes, as Christians, I believe we miss opportunities to have eternal impacts because we neglect to do the small things that could show people that we love them and that, in turn, Christ loves them. Most of us don't have the resources to do big or major things for people, but we all have the resources to say something encouraging to someone when they need lifting up; we all have the ability to say a "small" prayer for someone or send them a card or just tell them that we love them. I had an opportunity to encourage a friend recently who asked for prayer and was just feeling down. First, I prayed and then I sent her these words that God gave me for her:

Having a rough day
Is sometimes okay.
Just know that in time
It will all be fine.
You've asked me to pray
And I just did.
Remember that from Him
Nothing is hid.
He sees your tears
And I do too.
Please know that inside
I'm crying with you.
Look ahead to tomorrow
And lose that frown.
Cause the sun will come up
Or the Son will come down.

Matthew 13:32; John 6:9; Galatians 5:9.

❧ 8 ❧

THE ROOT PROBLEM

My grandson Levi was looking for odd jobs that he could do to help raise money to pay his way for our annual mission trip to Alaska with GraceWorks. The flower beds around our house needed weeding bad, so I told Levi that I would give him some money to help me pull weeds. It was a hot and humid day in May and the weeds were difficult to pull up out of the ground because the ground was dry. It was hard work.

After an hour or so of working, Levi said "I wish this would go faster." I told him that if we took our time and did it right the first time, making sure that we pulled up all the roots as we went, that we would never have to pull these same weeds again. I explained to him that if we didn't get the roots, the weeds would come back, and we would have to pull them over and over. Each time, the weeds would be more difficult to pull because the roots would get stronger and stronger. Levi understood what I was saying, but being a young boy, he still wanted to hurry up and get finished so he could collect his money.

God usually reveals things to me in unusual places and this was no exception—in a flower bed full of weeds, He was about to give me a lesson. I began to think about sin. Like weeds, if we don't get rid of sin in our lives, root and all, we will end up asking for forgiveness for the same sins over and over. Each time the sin will have a stronger hold on us, and it will be more difficult to get rid of. Getting rid of the roots of our sin requires true repentance, an act of turning away from it. If we ask forgiveness, our Father will forgive us but if we commit the same offenses over and over, the roots of those sins get stronger every time. If we ask our Father for forgiveness, in true repentance, and turn away from sin, the roots die with the sin.

The Bible has much to say about the root of sin. We know that satan sinned and that Eve sinned. Maybe they were two of the most famous sinners. What they both had in common was that their sins were rooted in pride and self-centeredness. Scripture tells us that the love of money is a root of all evil but studying all of God's Word clearly reveals to us that pride/love of self, is the root of sin. Rejecting God's will and doing our own will is the very definition of sin. We sin because we seek our own desires. That is the ultimate definition of pride. To get rid of the roots of sin in our lives, we must get ourselves out of the way.

God gave me the words to this song several years ago as I was looking at myself in the mirror. I saw so much self-centeredness in my own life. As I began to look at what I had prioritized as being the important things, I didn't like what I saw. Perhaps some of you can relate.

Less of Me

Got a hundred trophies hanging on the wall,
Got some money in the closet down the hall;
That doesn't mean anything at all.
Got a big ole house and yard to call my own,
Got a thousand minutes on my brand-new phone;
That doesn't mean anything at all.

Less of me, Lord open up my eyes that I might see
More of You, in everything I say and everything I do
Less of me, and more of You.

Got a good paying job down at the factory,
Got a healthy pension, one day, coming to me;
That doesn't mean anything at all.
Got the latest movie out on DVD,
Got a million channels on my big TV;
That doesn't mean anything at all.

Less of me, Lord open up my eyes that I might see
More of You, in everything I say and everything I do
Less of me, and more of You.

I must decrease and You must increase.
I must decrease and You must increase.
I must decrease and You must increase.
I must decrease and You must increase.

Less of me, Lord open up my eyes that I might see
More of You, in everything I say and everything I do
Less of me, and more of You.

> **Proverbs 13:10; Isaiah 30:1;**
> **Galatians 5:19–21; Romans 1:29–31.**

ᴈ 9 ᴇ

COMMUNICATION
BREAKDOWN

B efore I begin this story, I want to set the stage and make sure that everyone understands that this took place in a much different time than we live in today. Yes, looking back, I can find many problems with what transpired. There were definitely safety issues that were not thought out at the time. Kids were allowed to do things back in those days that we wouldn't consider letting our kids do today. I'm not going to argue, here, about whether that's a good thing or a bad thing. My parents loved me and would never have done anything or allowed me to do anything that they thought would hurt me. It was just different, period.

I was twelve- or thirteen-years-old at the time. My Daddy asked if I wanted to go riding over to an adjacent farm and see if we could jump up a covey of quail and maybe shoot a couple for supper that night. He didn't have to ask but one time and I was in the truck with my .410 single barrel shotgun that I had bought with my own money. I bought the gun for $45 when I was ten-years old. I had worked an entire season in the tobacco field for that $45. Daddy came out to the truck with his 12-gauge shotgun, and we drove over to the farm.

Whether or not we found any quail to shoot, I just don't remember. I do know that we walked all over the fields and I was excited. I also know that we didn't have any quail so if we shot at any we must have missed. After a while, it was time to go home.

What happened next was a series of poor decisions on mine and Daddy's part. I'm sure these decisions were brought on mostly by my nagging and they came very close to being life altering, catastrophic, and devastating. First, I loaded up in the back of the truck. In those days it was very common for kids to ride in the bed of trucks, especially when riding on farm roads. Secondly, I had the gun in my hands, and it was still loaded. Again, not a safe thing to do and a very poor decision, but not uncommon in that day and time. You see, I was still excited about the possibility of maybe seeing something to shoot for supper. When riding on farm paths it was common to see a covey of quail cross in front of you or a dove, rabbit, or squirrel. To be honest, I just wanted to shoot at something. Lastly, Daddy and I had not discussed my intentions or what I would do if I did see wild game to shoot at. Obviously, neither of us were using our brains at all.

We were riding along slowly when I spotted a rabbit sitting just in the edge of the woods. I didn't think

Daddy saw it but then he began to come to a stop. I was filled with anticipation and excitement. I was about to get to shoot a rabbit for supper. I raised my gun, pulled the hammer back and aimed. Just as I was pulling the trigger, the door opened, and my daddy stepped out of the truck all in one motion. As the gun went off, I could see Daddy in my peripheral vision. The gun barrel was less than a foot to the left of his head. In a fraction of a second, the gun fired, the rabbit was dead, Daddy and I both were in shock and I honestly thought I had shot Daddy.

When I first saw the rabbit, my first thought was to knock on the back window of the truck so that Daddy would stop. When he began to stop anyway, I thought that he had seen the rabbit but, in actuality, he had not seen the rabbit and was stopping to relieve himself. Yes, he had to pee, and I had no idea. Looking back, I guess he could have just told me out of his window that he was going to stop because he had to pee. Neither of us had communicated to the other what our intentions were. That was very nearly a tragedy that I don't even like to think about. It gives me cold chills to consider what almost happened just because of a few poor decisions but mainly because of poor communication.

Poor communication, incorrect communication, incomplete communication, or not communicating at all can cause many problems in our relationships with others, it can affect how we accomplish group tasks, and it can lead to dangerous consequences. Communication breakdown can also affect our spiritual walk and our witness.

God's Word gives us direction on how to communicate, what to communicate, and gives us forewarning of the result of proper communication and improper communication. We are told in Scripture that we should be reliable in our communication which brings healing. We have the choice to speak kindness and love or hate and anger. We are told that we will be held accountable for every word we speak and that the tongue is an instrument that can bring death or life. Every word that comes from our mouths is like a speeding bullet that we can't take back once we have fired the gun (our tongue). As hunters, hopefully, we wouldn't take a bad or unethical shot or just fire aimlessly into the woods. As Christians, hopefully, our aim is true when we speak to others. Our words should encourage and rebuke in Christlike love. It's like one of my supervisors told me a long time ago, "it's not always what you say but how you say it." I had to learn that one the hard way.

I have heard it said that God gave us one mouth and two ears for a reason. We should listen at least twice as much as we speak. God's Word says that it is shameful and foolish to speak before listening to the facts. I've heard it said also of people, especially politicians, that they would be okay if they would just keep their mouths shut. That's probably been said of me a time or two, honestly. When we do speak, we would do well to speak as Jesus did when He was here on earth. Communicating Jesus is what we should be about. Say His name.

> Proverbs 13:17; 18:13, 21; James 1:19;
> Matthew 12:36; 1 Corinthians 14:9.

✄ 10 ✄

UNORTHODOX METHODS

I t was one of those April days when everything was just perfect for fishing. The temperature was in the mid-70s and there was a gentle westerly breeze. My Granddaddy had a saying that "when the wind is out of the west, the fish bite the best and when it's out of the east, the fish bite the least." I have certainly found this to be true over the years. My mother, or Mama as I called her, my son Shane and myself were at our favorite fishing hole. The crappies were spawning, and we were catching them on almost every cast. We were fishing from the bank and the wind was blowing the warmest water to one side of the pond. There was a small boat dock sticking out into the water and the fish seemed to be congregating near it.

We were casting mini jigs and slowly retrieving them. This was not a catch and release fishing trip but rather a "fish fry" fishing trip. We planned to keep enough fish for a family fish fry. We were catching some really nice crappie and occasionally a small one. We released the small ones back into the pond to be caught when they grew up. It seemed that almost every time we were reeling a small crappie in near the boat dock, a huge bass would come up and try to grab it. After about the third time, it got my attention.

I quickly turned my focus from crappie fishing to bass fishing. This was no ordinary bass. I started casting a white, inline spinner bait with my bait caster thinking that if that big ole bass was trying to grab crappie, this spinner bait would catch it. I made what seemed like a hundred casts to no avail. I tried several other bass lures, but the bass wasn't interested. Meanwhile, my son was reeling in another small crappie when the bass lunged at it again. I thought about using a crappie for bait, but I didn't have any large hooks with me. I was getting frustrated that I couldn't trick this bass into biting one of the big bass lures. Finally, I got tired of trying and started back crappie fishing.

I cast the tiny crappie jig out in the same spot that I had been throwing the bass lures and something hit it. I immediately knew that this wasn't a crappie. The drag on my reel began to sing and line was peeling off rapidly. My first thought was that I would never get this fish in with this tiny hook and 6 lb. test fishing line. Mama grabbed her camera and started taking pictures of the fight. I still have those pictures today. Keep in mind that we didn't have cell phones back then to take videos with. As the bass went from one end of the pond to the other, I walked back and forth on the bank. Not wanting to put too much pressure on my line or the hook, I let the fish slowly tire herself out. Finally, after several minutes of fighting the bass, I landed her. We weighed her and the scales showed ten pounds. A ten-pound bass in our neck of the woods is a really big fish. I decided that she was going to the taxidermist and ultimately on my wall. I couldn't believe that I had just caught a ten-pound bass on a tiny crappie jig. Proven methods didn't work on this big bellied lunker.

As I reflect on the memories of that day, I have a flood of emotions. I'm thankful for that time of joy that I was able to share with my son and my Mama. They were my cheerleaders as I was fighting that fish. I was teasing my Mama about taking the pictures. She always had her camera and took pictures of everything. I'm so glad now that I have those pictures. My Mama, and her camera, reminds me of something that my friend Barney told me. He said that when he was a kid, his Mama took so many pictures with a flash camera that every time that a thunderstorm came up and there was a streak of lightning, he and his brother would smile. It was about like that with my Mama too.

That unorthodox fishing experience has taught me much about how I need to be witnessing to others when I'm trying to lure them or "catch them" for Christ. First, I believe that the #1 most successful witness is how we live our lives every day. What others see in us and how we handle life are our greatest witnesses. Knocking on doors works at times but I'm not a door knocker. Passing out Christian tracts can be successful, but it seems that it hasn't worked very well for me. Other traditional witnessing techniques just haven't seemed to be very effective for me.

In Alaska, the seeds that our mission teams have planted have grown into much fruit, not due to traditional methods, but in doing exactly what Christ has commanded us. We don't go to Alaska screaming Jesus, we go there and just love people in tangible ways. If they are hungry, we feed them. If they are naked, we clothe them. If they are homeless, we try to find them shelter. If they are lonely, we befriend them. If they need a hug, we give them one. If they are abusers, we offer them hope and alternatives. When they ask us why we are doing this, we tell them because we love them. When they ask us why we love them, we tell them because Jesus first loved us. Although some have come to salvation and been baptized, we don't always catch them (lead them to Christ) but we always get their attention. That's the first step in catching a fish and the first step in catching a soul—a tiny lure, a tiny act of love, a giant bass—a huge eternal implication.

The lyrics below are from a song that I wrote in 2012. I was thinking about how I needed to be witnessing and God told me plainly that it was in my everyday life. I had a story to tell and He wanted me to tell it with my words and my actions.

What's Your Story?

Jesus said for us to go and be fishers of men
But sometimes we don't know how to go in the midst of
all our sin.
This question's running through our minds again and again,
How do we witness in the world we're living in?

We talk and talk and try and try,
But people turn away
Until they see it in our lives.
There's nothing we can say.
We need to talk the talk and walk the walk
Each and every day.
Then when we look into our Father's eyes
"Well done," He will say.

It's in your actions, in your story
In your giving God all the glory.
It's in the way you live and how you give
How you spend your time and your sacrifice.
What's your story?
I wanna hear your story.
You gotta tell your story.
What's your story?

A new creation is our claim,
But where's the evidence?
People won't believe our claim

If we're riding on the fence.
If double minded seeds are sown
No fruit will come our way;
There won't be many workers there
On the harvest day.

It's in your actions, in your story,
In your giving God all the glory.
It's in the way you live and how you give,
How you spend your time and your sacrifice.
What's your story?
Tell me your story.
Wanna hear your story.
What's your story?

> Matthew 4:19; 5:16: 9:37–38;
> I Peter 3:15; John 13:34.

11

SHOCK FACTOR

rowing up on a farm certainly taught me many
lessons about life that I have never forgotten.
One of those lessons came one day as I was walking
in the cow pasture with my cousins. We always had
barbed wire fencing surrounding our pasture, but as the
fencing needed replacing, we slowly began to use electric fencing. I was totally unfamiliar with exactly how
electric fencing worked and oblivious to the shock that
could result from contacting it. That all changed on that
day. My cousins began to coerce me to do something
that was probably about the dumbest thing I would ever
do. They told me to pee on the fence to see what it
would do. Being a kid, I had no idea about electricity
and how it would transfer through moisture, which in
this case was pee and it was attached to me. You get the
picture. After they dared me a couple of times, which
was serious to kids back in those days, I succumbed to
the peer pressure and let er rip. I didn't know many cuss
words back then, but I'm sure I said all the ones I did

know. Of course, my cousins were hysterical. It certainly wasn't funny to me. To say it was shocking would be to put it way too mildly for sure.

The electric fencing worked well for most of our cows, but there was always one or two that would manage to get through it. I'm not sure if they were just tough or whether they were suckers for misery. Either way, after the initial shock or two, they would go through the fencing like it didn't even have an electric charge. Sometimes, we would increase the amperage on the fence. That would work on some of the stubborn cows, but some of them would still manage to get out of the fence. When these cows were no longer shocked and continued to get out of the fence, they were in danger of becoming our beef for the winter. We had too much to do on the farm to deal with chasing cows every day. You could say that these rogue cows had lost their shock factor.

Fast-forward to about forty years later: A major snowstorm, at least for our part of the country, had dumped about ten feet of snow on the landscape. The wind was howling, and it was very cold. My wife and I rarely get to stay at home together and just relax so we both took a couple of vacation days from work. Inside, it was warm, and we had some good snacks. I was channel surfing on the TV and came across a show that we had never seen before. I won't mention the title of the show, but it sounded interesting. Also, there was a marathon all day for this show. So, we settled in with our snacks, all cozy, and began to watch the first episode. It didn't take very long for my wife and I to look at each other and say, "what in the world kind of show is this?" We both had our mouths hanging open in shock at what we were seeing. There were all sorts of things going on that we just weren't accustomed to seeing on TV. I won't name them all, but about every sin you can think of was being portrayed by these actors and actresses on this show. My wife and I were both in shock at the things we were seeing. I probably said, "can you believe this?" a hundred times during this first episode.

Looking back, I should have turned the channel after the first few minutes of watching this garbage, but I didn't. We grabbed another snack in anticipation of the next episode. As we began to watch another episode, we were still shocked at what we were seeing. However, after a few episodes, we were no longer shocked by what we were seeing but were expecting it. What had our mouths hanging open a couple of hours earlier was now just becoming normal. It seems as if we had adjusted to the shock just like those rogue cows had with our electric fence years earlier. We had accepted that these sins would be a part of this show. After a few more episodes, we both had seen enough.

What transpired on that snowy day led to this revelation from God. When we are no longer shocked by something, it starts to become normal. The first step in acceptance of something is no longer being shocked by it.

I believe that in our world today we have lost our shock factor over the appalling things that are becoming more and more accepted in our society. As Christians, we must never lose sight of the fact that what was sin when God's Word was written is still sin today. We need to stay shocked. If we are shocked, we will be more likely to go and do something about the ugliness in our world. If we are no longer shocked, we accept, and God can't use us in the midst of sin's acceptance.

Ephesians 5:11; Jeremiah 2:12.

12

A TRUE TROPHY

I t seems that it's the same people every year who grace the covers of the outdoor magazines. The same faces show up year after year on social media with their record book bucks, huge gobblers, or humongous fish. I've wondered how and why the same people seem to be so successful. I've heard it said that the sun doesn't shine on the same dog's hind end every day but sometimes it really does seem like it. It can be frustrating to do everything correctly, put in your time and still not have the success that others seem to have on a consistent basis. I'm not taking away from the effort that some sportsmen and sportswomen have put in or the skills that they have, but it just doesn't seem fair sometimes. I've been able to harvest some decent whitetail bucks over the years but never anything that would make any of the record books. I've caught some really nice bass and killed turkeys with long beards and spurs but again, nothing that really stands out as being a true trophy according to the record books or the magazines.

As I dwell on outdoor memories as recent as yesterday, I visualize in my mind many trophies. All of the firsts with my children and grandchildren: their first fish, deer, squirrel, or turkey was surely a trophy at the time. My Daddy's first and only buck of his lifetime, a spike, was a trophy to him and me and to my son who was sitting in the deer stand with him when he shot it. I have trophy recollections of the wonderful spring days fishing with my Mama and my grandparents. The warm sunshine on my face on a bitterly cold, winter morning sitting in a tree is a trophy. The smiles on the kids' faces that I've been fortunate enough to take hunting and fishing are trophies that will never be seen on the cover of a magazine but are some of the most special trophies to me. Just the opportunity to enjoy God's amazing creation is a trophy every single day.

The outdoor industry in recent years has painted the picture that a trophy is measured in antler scores, fish weights, and lengths, beard and spur lengths, and the age of an animal. These trophy requirements can leave the average hunter or fisherman feeling as if they are sub-par. When a gobbler is coming in to your calls and your heart is about to beat out of your chest, it doesn't matter if he is two years old or five years old. When a buck comes in chasing a doe and is grunting, it doesn't matter if he is a spike or a 150" six-year-old stud. It doesn't really matter whether you shoot the buck or the doe. To a guy trying to put meat in the freezer for his family, that doe the spike is chasing could be a real trophy. Trophies should never be measured by numbers. They should be measured by memories, by how excited you were, by situations, and emotions.

Likewise, have you ever wondered why it sometimes seems as if the ungodly, the unjust, the unrighteous are so successful? Have you ever wondered why those who live for satan seem to prosper? I've surely wondered about these things on occasion.

Perhaps part of the answer to these questions lies within our definitions of success and prosperity. If we measure these things monetarily, materially, or socially we are missing the mark. These are worldly measures. Success and prosperity in the kingdom world are measured in things such as blessings, joy, peace, grace, mercy, faith, hope, and love. The greatest success measurement of all is the acceptance of the gift of salvation.

Our relationship with Jesus should be our greatest trophy. Whatever or whoever is your god before God will never bring forth all of the kingdom measurements listed above. If your priority, your #1 focus, your greatest treasure is anything or anyone other than the one and only living God, you cannot and will not prosper or be successful. True success and prosperity can only come through the risen Savior, Jesus Christ.

Matthew 6:20; 6:33; Exodus, 20:3.

⚞ 13 ⚟

LOST FOREVER

I tried to dial the number several times, but I was shaking so badly that I just couldn't. I took several deep breaths and said to myself, "you have to calm down." I finally managed to call my son Shane and whisper, "I just shot Blackie." I went over the details with him and told him to meet me at my house to help me track him. An hour earlier, I had sent Shane and my wife Johnsie a text saying, "I missed Blackie." I had gone from the gutter to the top of the mountain in a matter of one hour. Here's how it all began.

It was early April and I had installed a trail camera at one of my food plots to see if I could get any pictures of turkeys. Turkey season would be coming in soon and this was a good way to scout without spooking the birds that I hoped were on my property. After about a week, I went and got the SD card out of the camera. When I arrived back home to view the pictures on my computer, I had a couple of surprises. There were three nice gobblers using my food plot regularly and that was exciting.

The real surprise though, was several pictures of a buck that had begun to grow his new set of antlers.

This buck was the most beautiful deer I had ever seen. His face was almost black, and he had very unusual coloration around his eyes and ears. The bases of his antlers were huge, and I could tell that this was going to be a very special buck when his antlers matured. His entire body was very dark. He wasn't a melanistic deer. In other words, he wasn't totally black, but he was darker than any deer I had ever seen. I give the bucks on my property names according to their characteristics, and I immediately named this one Blackie. I continued to monitor Blackie via trail cameras all spring and summer. His antlers were growing quickly, and I could tell that my property was his home as I had pictures of him every day.

When September arrived, my anticipation of possibly getting a shot at Blackie with my bow consumed me. His antlers had matured into what I estimated would score between 140" and 150." He was a 10-pointer, with great mass, long main beams, good tine length and an inside spread of approximately 17"–18." If I could harvest him, he would be the biggest buck I had ever taken.

Finally, bow season arrived and I was pumped. I expected to see Blackie on the first day and arrived at my stand early. I saw several deer that evening, including a couple of nice bucks but no Blackie. That trend continued throughout the whole first week. I checked the trail camera on Sunday afternoon of the beginning of the second week. Blackie was coming in to my food plot every evening within thirty minutes after dark. I was worried that he had become totally nocturnal.

It was the middle of the second week of bow season. I climbed into my ladder stand and settled in for what I assumed would be another afternoon of watching multiple deer with no sighting of Blackie. At about 6:00 P.M., I caught movement out of the corner of my eye and started watching a parade of bachelor bucks walking out into the food plot. There were six bucks in all and when the last one stepped out, I immediately recognized him as being Blackie. He was almost majestic. It was as if he knew that he was the special one. The other bucks, two of them very nice, walked to within 20 yards of my stand and began to eat on the corn, clover, and apple buffet. Blackie stepped up to where they were and just looked at them. They all scattered and gave the special one full reign over his choice of food, the apples. Blackie was facing me at 20 yards. I would never take a head-on shot with a bow and arrow and I needed for him to turn broadside. One of the other bucks went to the mineral lick that I had enhanced with apple flavored minerals. I had video of Blackie running other deer off of the mineral lick on numerous occasions. Blackie turned and began to walk toward the mineral site. I drew my bow back. This would be a 20-yard shot and I was already visualizing putting my hands around those antlers.

Whether I didn't line up my peep sight or didn't anchor the release, I'll never know, but somehow, I missed the easy shot. All six of the bucks bounded off over the horizon. I was so caught up in the moment that I didn't do any of the things that I needed to do prior to releasing an arrow. I try to mentally check off things in my mind prior to releasing an arrow. I call it the P.A.S.S. check: Peep sight, Anchor, Steady, Shoot. Buck fever, overconfidence, counting my chickens before they hatched; they all played a role in missing Blackie. I was so dejected. This once in a lifetime opportunity had presented itself and I blew it. That's when I sent the text saying that I had missed.

I put another arrow on the rest and just sat there in disbelief. What had happened? How did I miss that chip shot? Would I ever see Blackie again? About an hour later, at approximately 7:00 P.M., I caught movement on the opposite end of the food plot. I couldn't believe what I was seeing. All six of the bucks had come back. They had made a big circle trying to get downwind of that strange noise that had spooked them an hour earlier. A huge 6-pointer that always stayed with Blackie walked right up to the corn pile and started eating. Blackie was at 35 yards, facing me and checking out his surroundings. He was timid and knew that something wasn't right. The other bucks came on in to the corn and apples, but Blackie remained at 35 yards. For what seemed like an eternity, Blackie never moved and was looking straight toward me. It was a standoff that had me about to come unglued. I know my knees were shaking, my heart was pounding, and I couldn't believe this was happening. I had read stories about people getting second chances, but it had never happened to me. Finally, Blackie turned and offered me a slight quartering away shot at 35 yards. I aimed for the opposite side lung, which meant I had to shoot a little further back than if he was broadside. I released the arrow. I heard the thump that confirmed that I had not missed. That's when I started shaking violently and tried to call Shane.

I got down from the stand at dark and walked back home. I was smiling when I walked in. My wife was expecting to hear my sob story I'm sure. I had not informed her about anything beyond the miss. I shared the story with her in excitement. I couldn't wait for Shane to arrive so we could begin the tracking process. I gathered my flashlights and extra batteries.

Shane arrived and we began tracking. It had been about two hours since the shot and I felt comfortable that I had made a good shot. I was also concerned that coyotes would find Blackie first. We found good blood immediately, but we couldn't find my arrow. That should have been an indication that the arrow had not passed completely through. I was so excited however, and the blood was so good, that we continued tracking. The tracking job was easy, as there was a lot of blood. We fully expected to find Blackie at any time. We followed the blood trail down to the creek and saw where Blackie had exited the creek on the other side. We continued to follow the trail when we came up on a barbed wire fence that connects my property with the neighbor's property. I have permission to try and recover wounded animals from the landowner, so we proceeded. When Blackie jumped the fence, it should have indicated to me that I needed to back out and wait until morning, but the blood was still good, so we continued on. After about another 100 yards, the blood trail started to get difficult to follow. Blackie was not bleeding profusely any longer. There were only small specks of blood. We came to a wooded bottom in the middle of a pasture and couldn't find any more blood. We looked and looked but couldn't find any blood beyond that point. I was starting to get concerned at that point.

We backed out and I contacted a handler who has blood tracking dogs. It took about two hours for the handler to arrive with the dog. We began at the beginning of the blood trail and the dog tracked the blood all the way to the point where Shane and I had lost it. The dog couldn't find anything else. We decided to wait until morning and bring another dog in to try and find Blackie. I didn't sleep any the rest of that night and was eager to hopefully pick up the trail the next morning and find Blackie. When the second dog lost the blood trail at the same point that Shane and I and the first dog had lost it, my heart sank. The second dog did find about 8" of my arrow with the broadhead still attached underneath the leaves right where we had lost the blood trail. We looked and looked and let the dog work for a couple of hours to no avail. I was thinking to myself that if it was a mortal wound and Blackie was dead maybe the buzzards would show me where he was in the next few days.

I spent countless hours the next few days walking and looking for any sign or for buzzards but never found anything. I went to the last spot of blood and went in every direction possible but nothing. I lost a lot of sleep; I was upset and I'm sure that I wasn't very pleasant company for anyone for quite a while after that. I half-heartedly hunted for the rest of the season with no luck. I monitored my trail cameras but never had another picture of Blackie. I was hoping that he survived. I put the word out for other hunters in the area to be on the lookout for his remains or if he was alive, to share a sighting or picture. When deer season was over in January, I began to walk every day in the woods, in the creek, everywhere I could think of, to try and find Blackie. I spent countless hours and walked many miles in rough terrain but never found Blackie. It finally hit me that Blackie was lost forever.

A long while after, I was thinking about all that had transpired, and God revealed something to me that put things back into perspective. What if I had expended as much energy into trying to win lost souls as I had to try and recover a lost deer. What if I lost sleep over people's lostness like I did over a lost animal? What if I was as concerned about lost sheep as I was a lost whitetail. I can only imagine the implication of the kind of desire I had to recover Blackie being funneled into the desire to bring people out of their lostness and into the arms of Jesus. I can only imagine the fruit and the harvest of exhausting all means to try and bring people to Jesus like I did when trying to find Blackie. What if I stayed the course when people said no to Jesus and kept trying to witness to them like I stayed in the stand after I had missed Blackie? I never want to lose another deer like I did Blackie, but it has become much more important to me not to lose anyone in my family, my friends, anyone at all to an eternal hell.

Luke 15:4.

14

I Asked for It

D awn was about to make its appearance. The birds were waking up. All around me were the sounds of an approaching new day. Somewhere on the opposite side of my property, a barred owl pierced the stillness with his *whoo whoo whoo whoo.... whoo whoo whoo whoo.* A thunderous gobble followed, then another double gobble. I started making my way through the woods in the direction the gobbles had come from. My anticipation was building with every step. I knew I had to hurry and get set up on this bird before he flew down. I assumed this ole Tom turkey was roosted near the creek. I stopped a couple of hundred yards from the creek and let out my own owl hoot. My *whoo whoo whoo whoo.... whoo whoo whoo whoo* was cut off by a double gobble. I wasn't sure if there were two birds or if there was only one that was so fired up, he was double gobbling. To my dismay, the birds, or bird, had roosted on the other side of the creek on property that I had not secured permission to hunt on.

Calling a turkey across a creek is not an easy task or one that happens very often, but I had been able to entice a few across barriers in my years of hunting. I set up about 30 yards from the creek and about 100 yards down the creek from where the gobbler was roosted. I placed my decoy close to the creek. I got my slate call out of the holder, put my diaphragm (mouth) call in my cheek and tried to visualize exactly where I might get a shot if this ole boy decided to come in to my calls. All the while, the old great thunderchicken was gobbling at everything. The owls were really cranked up all around and one of the neighboring farmers was plowing a field off in the distance. The high-pitched sounds of the plow hitting rocks in the field were driving the gobbler crazy. As turkey hunters like to put it, he was hot to trot.

I started yelping very softly with my mouth call, and he very politely answered back each time. He was definitely interested in this fake hen. Then, I started clucking with my slate call and took my hat off and beat it against my knee mimicking the fly down sounds of a hen. Then I started a series of purrs and yelps, letting him know that this fake hen had hit the ground and was ready for action. He gobbled and gobbled. It seemed as if he gobbled 100 times or more. Then I heard the distinct sound of this ole boy flying down off the roost. I began to think, *"this just might happen."*

I could tell that he had walked or strutted down to the creek. He was getting closer and closer. I could hear him walking on the sandbar in the creek. One thing was for sure, nobody owned the middle of the creek, so if he came in walking on a sandbar, I could legally shoot him. Or perhaps, he would come across the creek. I was trembling and my heart was about to explode as I heard his footsteps in the sand about 20 yards up the creek. I couldn't see him due to the dense undergrowth along the bank of the creek. He would have to get right in front of me before I could see him. He had stopped gobbling which is normal when they are approaching and looking for a hen. I remember saying a quick prayer: "Lord please let him come on in and let it be a big bird."

I could hear him getting closer and closer. At this point, I was about to come unglued. I knew this was about to happen. Then I caught a glimpse of his beak, just a tiny glimpse. My safety was off, and my finger was on the trigger. As soon as he took a couple more steps, I would be able to see him clearly and take the shot. All of a sudden, he came into view. But wait, what the heck? It wasn't a turkey at all. It was a 4' tall blue heron walking in the creek fishing for minnows. My heart went from explode mode to sinking ship mode in a fraction of a second. I remember thinking *"you've got to be kidding me."*

I smile when I think back on this turkey hunting memory. It's hilarious to me now but it surely wasn't funny that day. I can only imagine that as all of this was unfolding, that big ole gobbler was probably standing 20 yards behind me wondering why that camouflage blob was making hen sounds directed toward that blue heron. If turkeys can laugh, I'm sure that one did. I couldn't help but recall what I had prayed for, that it would be a big bird and that it would come on in. Well, I thought to myself, *"God answered my prayer exactly the way I prayed it."*

My lesson on that day was that I need to be more specific when I pray. I find myself on many occasions praying for my family, friends, and others by name but until I began to pray specific things for them, it didn't seem as if God was giving me answers to my prayers. In reality, I didn't know whether he was answering them or not because I had not prayed for specific needs or specific issues for those people. I have prayed for our world, our nation, and our leaders often but failed to pray specifically. I should have been praying that our nation would turn back to God, that our leaders would look to Him for guidance and act accordingly.

I am reminded of the story of the blind beggars calling out to Jesus for mercy. They were persistent, but their prayers were too general. Jesus didn't answer their prayers. They remained blind. Then Jesus asked them what exactly it was that they wanted him to do. When they specifically told Him that they wanted to receive their sight, Jesus healed them and gave them their sight. Quite often I pray that God will "be with" or "help" a particular individual. What He wants me to pray is "be with" that person or "help" that person because of, or for the specific issue that they are dealing with. My prayer life became meaningful and I started getting answers when I began to pray specifically. God used that failed turkey hunt on that morning to teach me how to pray and gave me a few laughs too.

Matthew 20:29–34.

15

YOU ARE MY BROTHER

T rail cameras have revolutionized the hunting industry. There's no doubt about that. I started using them years ago when you had to put film in them. I remember the first time I ever used one. I put the camera on a tree overlooking a field where I suspected a big buck was roaming. I checked the camera a few days later and was excited to find out that the camera was full. I took the film to a drug store to have it developed. I chose the more expensive, one hour option. I couldn't wait to see what my trail camera had captured. An hour later, I picked up the pictures, and while I was paying for them, the clerk was giggling. I was so embarrassed when I opened the envelope and looked at the pictures right there at the counter. I had an entire roll of film's worth of a weed blowing back and forth in the wind. Well, I learned something that day anyway. Trail cameras have come a long way since then. Soon there were cameras that were infrared and had the date, time, and moon phase when each picture was taken. They used

SD cards and there was no more going to the drug store for developing. I am thankful for that. Those are the cameras that I still use, but the latest technology offers cameras that work off satellites and send the pictures to your cell phone.

I generally keep several cameras running on my property year-round. I enjoy capturing all kinds of wildlife. You never know what's going to be on the SD card. I've even captured pictures of a few trespassers over the years. The biggest reason I run the trail cameras when there is no hunting season in is to judge the condition of the deer herd and the turkey flock. With diseases spreading across the country, it's important to keep up with the size and physical condition of the deer herd. It's also important to try and determine if there was a good or bad turkey hatch in the spring. If the deer or turkey population is down, I try to determine whether the decline is habitat related, disease related, or whether there is too much predation from coyotes or hunting pressure. By monitoring the trail cameras year-round, I can reasonably judge the steps I need to take to maintain the overall condition of the wildlife on my property.

I believe that we, as Christians, have to be able to judge the overall condition of the souls of people. That includes our brothers and sisters in Christ when they stumble as well as those who are lost. I know, I know, I know. The Bible says, "judge not." Matthew 7:1 "Judge not that you be not judged" is one of the most quoted verses of Scripture by Christians and non-Christians.

It is also one of the most misunderstood Scriptures. It is used most often as an excuse to either get a fellow brother or sister off one's back or by a nonbeliever to silence a witness. In other words, it is used most of the time as a defense mechanism.

There is only one true judge when it comes to judging people and souls and His name is Jesus. However, when it comes to judging the condition of people, we all, as Christians, have that responsibility. In John 7:24 Jesus says, "stop judging by mere appearances, but instead judge correctly." We should be there to help our brothers and sisters get back up when they fall. We are required to tell them, in love, when it is obvious that there is sin in their lives. That's not my opinion, it's a command from God. How can we possibly do that if we don't know their condition? We also have a responsibility to witness to the lost. Jesus said that He would make us fishers of men, if we follow Him. How can we possibly fish for men if we don't know who is already hooked on Jesus? A fisherman needs to know where to concentrate his efforts on a large body of water so as not to waste too much time and energy in unproductive areas. Likewise, fishers of men need to know where to concentrate their witnessing efforts in a mighty big world. We need to become masters of judging the condition of people's souls. We need to go after the lost and hold up the saved.

Below are the lyrics God gave me for a song about accountability. I wrote this song in honor of a very special brother, Eric Hardman. Eric was our youth minister at the time. He came to me one day and asked if I would consider being his accountability partner. I told him I sure would if he would tell me what an accountability partner was. Basically, we came together for a few minutes each week to talk about the struggles we both had encountered during the week, prayed for each other about these matters, and suggested solutions for each other. I had never had anyone point things out to me, about me, in love before. My experience with accountability had been people gossiping about me or flat out telling me, bluntly and hatefully, about my failures. It was difficult at first, but I quickly learned how to accept and give constructive criticism and learned how to be wrong. I found out that the truth of the matter is that it's alright to be wrong as long as you learn and grow from it.

You Are My Brother

Watch over me and I'll watch over you.
It's our responsibility
I'm holding you accountable.
Please do the same for me.
It's not that I think that we should be each other's judge,
That job's reserved for our Father up above.

Don't let me stumble, my brother.
Help keep me strong.

Help me stay humble, my brother.
Tell me when I am wrong.
You are my brother.

I ask that you don't talk about me.
I'll do the same in return.
Please come to me constructively,
With love and concern.
Our goal should be the same if we are both in Christ.
Please do not be ashamed, I welcome your advice.

Don't let me stumble, my brother.
Help keep me strong
Help me stay humble, my brother
Tell me when I am wrong.
You are my brother.

We live in a day and time when we don't hold others accountable and we don't like to be held accountable. We don't love others enough to judge their condition and we don't want our condition judged. We only see people as that weed blowing back and forth in the wind. We don't see the disease of sin, the predation of satan, or the poor habitat that people live in. It could be that we don't want to hear them quote "judge not," or it could be that we just don't care.

Matthew 7:1–3; James 5:16;
Ezekiel 33:8; Galatians 6:1–2.

⚜ 16 ⚜

Didn't See That Coming

I t was mid-October, and the October lull was in full swing. It seemed as if all the deer on earth had vanished. I was sitting in a tree with my bow hoping that today would be the day that things changed. After all, the rut was only three weeks away and the bucks should start chasing does any day. I was sitting in a ladder stand that was strapped to a big cedar overlooking a small food plot. I had killed several nice bucks from that stand in years past. I was ready for a 20- or 30-yard shot with my bow. I had practiced those shots over and over because every deer I had ever harvested from that stand had offered me broadside shots at those distances. I had not seen anything but squirrels all afternoon and darkness was only one hour away. That last hour of daylight has historically been prime time for me.

I glimpsed something coming through the woods from my right. I couldn't tell what it was at first, but I thought it was a coyote or a dog. Then it stepped out of the woods. It was a huge bobcat. At first, I thought it was a mountain lion, but I'd never heard of a mountain lion in my neck of the woods and it didn't have a tail. I had only seen one bobcat in my life prior to this. I had a couple of trail camera images of a big cat, but I didn't realize that he was this big. Bobcats are ferocious predators, and I could only imagine how many rabbits and fawns this one had killed and eaten off my property. He was approaching an open spot on the edge of the food plot that would place him at 5 yards from my tree stand. I drew my bow back. Having only one sight pin on my bow that was set at 20 yards, I knew that I would have to aim low in order to hit the cat. When he entered the opening, I let the arrow fly. The bobcat jumped straight up in the air and just stood and looked around when he landed. I had shot just underneath him and was trying desperately to nock another arrow. The bobcat casually walked away and actually sat down in front of my trail camera. I have some awesome close-up pictures of him but I couldn't get another shot at him. He eventually went back in the woods. I was shaking and upset that I had missed him. The rest of the evening was uneventful. At dark, I retrieved my dirt covered arrow and walked home to share the story with my wife.

I replayed the events of that day over and over in my head for the next few days. I practiced shooting from 5 and 10 yards with my bow. I realized that I had overcompensated with my sight and that's why I shot too low. If this situation presented itself again, I would be ready.

The bottom line is that I missed this once in a lifetime opportunity because I wasn't prepared.

Quite honestly, I would have a difficult time believing this next story if I had not experienced it firsthand. I've shared it with family members and a few friends and the look on their faces led me to believe that they were a little concerned about my mental stability. It's actually so bizarre that I couldn't have made it up. I don't have that kind of imagination.

It was two weeks after I had missed the huge bobcat. It was the first afternoon of primitive weapons season or what I call muzzleloader season. I had hunted that morning out of a different stand and had heard some chasing and grunting back toward my ladder stand in the cedar tree, so I decided that's where I would spend the afternoon. There is an old logging road that leads to my stand. On either side of the logging road was broom straw that stood about 3' tall. As I was approaching my stand, I heard something moving around in the broom straw. As I was looking for what made the sound, I saw the broom straw moving and I knew something was there, but I couldn't see anything. Then 20 yards away, I saw a bobcat walk through a small opening in the broom straw. My heart began to race. I was thinking to myself that I wished he would come back to that opening. Then another bobcat walked past the opening. I couldn't believe that I had just seen two bobcats. Of course, I could no longer see either one of them. Then, as if I had written the script, a third bobcat stepped into the opening and just stood there. I was using an in-line, .50-caliber muzzleloader with a scope. I raised my gun, and I couldn't find the bobcat in my scope. I lowered the gun and could see him perfectly. I adjusted the scope setting down to 1 because the bobcat was only 20 yards away. When I raised the gun again, I still couldn't find the bobcat in my scope. I was about to have a heart attack. I lowered the gun and watched as the bobcat walked out of the open area and into the thick brush just like the other two cats had—another missed opportunity.

Then, as my brain was whirling and my heart about to beat out of my chest, I did something that to this day leaves me shaking my head when I think about it. For some insane reason, I began to make a dying rabbit sound with my mouth. In an instant, one of the bobcats crashed out of the thick brush and was leaping straight toward me. I threw the gun up and fired from the hip. I didn't have time to aim or get the gun to my shoulder. Of course, I missed. It seemed as if the bobcat turned in midair and landed only a few feet from me. If you're familiar with muzzleloaders, you know that you only have one shot and then you have to reload with powder and a bullet and install a firing cap. By the time, I even thought about reloading, the bobcat was gone. I've often thought about that day and how awesome it would have been to have those events on video. But the story doesn't end there.

Again, unpreparedness had left me unsuccessful. If I had only taken my pistol with me that day. I made up my mind that I was going to get one of those bobcats even if I had to give up my deer hunting for a few days. I had watched predator hunters on TV and had read a couple of articles about it, but I knew absolutely nothing about how to call in a bobcat. I knew that a decoy of some sort was supposed to help and that a dying rabbit call was a good call to use. I had a dying rabbit mouth call that I had purchased to try my hand at coyote hunting. I didn't have anything to use for a decoy, so I went to town looking for a stuffed animal of some kind. When the country boy goes to town, there just ain't no tellin' what might happen. I had read that using stuffed animals was a technique that some predator hunters had been successful with. I had in my mind that I needed something white. The only stuffed animal I could find in the store was, of all things, a unicorn. I felt really stupid, but I purchased the white stuffed unicorn.

This is where the story gets unbelievable and hilarious at the same time. I wouldn't blame anyone reading this for thinking that I made it up or that I'm a brick shy of a full load. Dressed in camouflage, and carrying my 12-gauge shotgun, a dying rabbit mouth call, and a white stuffed unicorn, I proceeded to go to my ladder stand in the middle of the day to try and persuade a bobcat into shotgun range. I know that visions of Ole Man Fudd are coming into some of your minds right now. I sat the stuffed unicorn down in the middle of the small food plot. I climbed up into my stand and began making a series of calls mimicking a dying rabbit. I probably sounded more like a dying cow in a hailstorm. Right after the third series of calls, as I was feeling pretty stupid for even attempting this ridiculousness, I saw movement out of my left eye. Something was coming down the logging road. I clicked the safety off on the shotgun as it was laying in my lap. I didn't dare move my head. I could see movement and it appeared to be brown or gray in color. Whatever it was seemed to be heading for the stuffed unicorn. I just knew I was about to get a shot at a bobcat. Then it stepped into view. I almost fell out of the tree when I realized that it was a deer with only one antler. It walked right up and sniffed the unicorn. I began to think to myself *"nobody is ever going to believe this."* I had successfully called in a unicorn using a unicorn as a decoy. As the deer walked away, I was laughing so hard that the tree stand was shaking. That was the last time I ever tried to call in a bobcat. I've never seen another one either.

I guess I was somewhat prepared, that day, for a bobcat to come in to my setup but I certainly wasn't prepared for a real live unicorn. God surely has a sense of humor.

More than ever before, we need to be prepared for what life throws at us or presents us with. We may need to make sure that we are prepared financially. Savings, 401Ks or retirement planning may help with that. In some cases, we need to be prepared for catastrophic events. Perhaps insurance policies can help with that. Sadly, we need to be prepared for the people that satan uses to terrorize and cause harm to others. Maybe locks, security systems, and legally packing defensive weapons can help with that. But none of these things truly matter if your heart isn't prepared. Only Jesus can help with that.

As Christians, we need to be ready for our Lord's return. Accepting the free gift of salvation is the first and foremost, mandatory preparation for eternal life. But it shouldn't end there for us. We should be helping others to prepare for that day also. When a bad storm such as a hurricane is forecasted to hit an area, people seem to help one another prepare for it by boarding up windows, clearing debris, and making other preparations. Why wouldn't we want to help our neighbor be prepared for judgement day? There are many ways we can do that such as showing Christlike love to people around us, but the main way is by sharing Jesus with them. Testifying about what God has done in our lives and how He saved us is the best way to help with preparing others for eternity. Scripture tells us that we should be prepared to give a reason for the hope that is in us. We should prepare by studying God's Word, not for the sake of arguing, but so that we can share "the truth." We should prepare by listening as God reveals things to us through His Word and through life events.

Not being prepared when hunting and fishing and in other aspects of life has cost me many times over the years, but I'm so thankful that I'll never have to worry about being unprepared for the end of my earthly life. Thank God, at thirty-three years of age, I took care of that.

Matthew 24:44; Proverbs, 6:6–8; 1 Peter 3:15.

⇥ 17 ⇤

DIVIDED WE FALL

When I was growing up in rural North Carolina, we had to depend on word of mouth for information about someone killing a big buck or catching a big fish. Most of the time, we heard about things such as that at the country store sitting around a wood stove. I used to love hearing some of the old timers talk about their adventures. No one ever asked what a fish weighed or how much a buck scored because they just didn't know. It was more about how much meat they supplied. With the creation and expanding opportunities of social media over the last few years, there are many hunting and fishing groups that a sportsman can participate in online. I became a member of several of those groups because I thought it would be interesting to see the deer people killed and the fish people caught. I never imagined when I joined these groups that much of what is posted or commented about is people voicing their opinions (mostly negative) about other sportsmen and women, and even kids, because of what they choose to harvest or how they choose to harvest it.

I assumed, wrongly, that most folks who enjoy hunting and fishing were somewhat like me and that they celebrated one another's success. I also assumed that we as sportsmen and women were a group that would stick together in unity against the anti-hunting and anti-right to bear arms groups. I quickly found out that there is great division amongst what I thought would be a tightly knit sportsman family. Whenever someone kills a monster buck or catches a huge fish, the first response from many is that it was done illegally. Jealousy and envy have taken the place of high fives and congratulatory gestures. I've seen comments condemning hunters, even kid hunters, for killing what was supposedly a deer that wasn't mature enough yet. I've read arguments about whether it's ethical to hunt over bait. The choice of weapons raises differing opinions. There are those who try to shame other hunters because they choose to use crossbows instead of traditional or compound bows. Another argument that has come on the scene in the last few years is whether it is ethical for fishermen to use the advanced fish finders and sonars that have been made available. All this division among what should be a huge sportsman family only gives fuel to those who wish to abolish our rights to hunt and fish. We all need to learn how to disagree without being critical of one another and to stand firmly together against those who have their sights set on taking away our God-given constitutional rights.

We are living in a time of great division in our nation. We seem to be divided over so many things such as race, ethnicity, and gender. We're divided about such ridiculous things as whose life matters the most. We're divided socially and politically. Almost every day there is another issue that we are pressured into taking sides on. Families are divided and friends are separated because they can't come to terms with having different opinions on issues. All of this division has made us, as a nation of people, extremely vulnerable to attack from the rest of the world. If we were asked to stand together in unity today, I'm afraid it would be a very difficult task. There should only be one true division amongst all the people of the world: whether you have or have not accepted the free gift of salvation through Jesus Christ. If we are on the saved side of that dividing line, we should be doing everything in our power to reach out and help people across that line.

Sadly, there is so much division even in the church and amongst believers nowadays that it is hard to recognize the church from the world. Believers argue over everything under the sun. I have been in church business meetings where there were hard feelings over things such as what color the new carpet needs to be. My Daddy used to say that it didn't matter whether Jesus rode a donkey or a jackass but that he had heard church people argue about even that. Believers are divided by denomination, segregation, discrimination, litigation, obligation, mitigation, administration, communication, confrontation, preoccupation, gratification, individuation, dramatization, organization, compensation, manipulation, exploitation, coordination, congregation, intoxication, annunciation, information, examination, negotiation, frustration, fascination, and altercation. Wow, that's a lot of division.

Like any group of people that ever existed, Christians are going to disagree about things. The problem lies in disagreeing to the point that it causes division in the church. Every church that has ever split did so because of a disagreement about something. We should be able to disagree about the carpet color, or whether or not to pave the parking lot, without it affecting our ministry and witness to the world. As long as we all agree that God's Word is the truth and that we should all be working toward the same goal, saving a lost world, we should be able to disagree about things and still move forward with God's work. Believers become unbelievable when others see us fighting amongst ourselves. The apostle Paul encouraged us, as believers, not to have any division among us, to be united in the same mind and judgment, and not to quarrel.

1 Corinthians 1:10–13; Titus 3:9–11; Luke 11:17; Jude 1:16–19: Mark 3:24–26.

⚞ 18 ⚟

ALL THE LEAVES ARE BROWN

M id October in the piedmont section of North Carolina is a beautiful time of transformation. The first frosts of the season have ripened the persimmons. The trees have mostly given up their harvests of acorns, walnuts, pecans, hickory nuts, crab apples, and wild pears. It's a season of change from greenery to gorgeous fall foliage and from hot to cooler temperatures. Some years the leaves are prettier than others and some years it gets cool earlier than others.

As I was fishing in my pond on one of these October days, I began to look around me at the beauty and wonder of the fall. The forest was laid out in front of me like a wonderful masterpiece that an artist had just painted. The reflection in the water, perfectly mirrored the surrounding beauty and gave it a slight shimmer. The leaves were an assortment of bright reds, brilliant yellows, orange, and some almost had a purple tint. There also were many that were still green and, yes, there were a few brown ones that had died. Although the temperature was only in the mid-70s, it seemed much warmer, and I was so ready for the cooler weather to finally arrive. It seemed as if summer just didn't want to say goodbye.

I began to ponder what God might say if He were to speak to me at that moment. What was the message in this beautiful fall painting that I could grasp and share? An hour or so earlier, as I was looking out of my back window, I had said to my wife that everything sure was pretty but that it would be so much prettier if all of the leaves would turn at the same time. That thought was a forerunner to what God was trying to reveal to me. There were so many green leaves that still had not changed. Now, I don't have anything against green but it's just not as pretty as the other vibrant colors that appear when the leaves change. It's almost as if the green leaves are resisting the change and just trying to hold on a little longer. Everything is amazingly beautiful, but it would be even more beautiful if all the leaves would change at the same time. Although many would disagree with me, I think it would be great if summer would give up its warmth a little quicker also. Here in North Carolina, fall is a time when we need air conditioning and heat in the same day, and 40°– 50° temperature swings within a day are not uncommon. It always leaves me wanting summer to give up and let the cool change take its place.

So how can we view this as a learning example as it relates to us as Christians? It's very clear to me now that I let God speak to me through the leaves and the weather, that many of us are like those resistant green leaves in the fall and the determined heat of late summer. You see, we tend to want to hang on to our old lives just a little bit. We often desire to hold on to a few things that prevent us from totally becoming a new creature in Christ. God's Word tells us that if we are in Christ, the new creation has come and that the old has gone and the new is here. It's a beautiful thing to see someone come to Christ. But that beauty isn't what it could or should be when we hold on to things that keep us from allowing God to make us a completely new creation.

It isn't my desire to change what the leaves do or the weather. That's all in God's will and control. It is my desire that every person becomes a completely new creation. One day all of the leaves will turn brown and die. Hopefully, the whole tree isn't dead and there will be new life come spring.

2 Corinthians 5:17; Ephesians 4:22–24; 1 Peter 2:24.

⚎ 19 ⚎

YOU MAY SAY
I'M A DREAMER

I was sitting 20 feet up in a tree. It was a rare occasion for me to be hunting on the small farm that I grew up on. I began to visualize, dream, or recall; I guess all three words fit the scenario. I could almost smell tobacco curing in the barn. I could just about hear and see my grandma, granddaddy, Mama and Daddy, even though they had all departed this earthly life. I could hear Daddy cranking up that Carolina blue '55 Chevy. Mama was cooking breakfast before leaving for work. I could see Grandma preparing lunch for everybody before meeting us all in the tobacco field. I recalled the stories that Granddaddy would tell about his youth and how he made me laugh. All the memories of my childhood were running through my head. With a smile on my face, I was brought back to reality as the sun began to rise. I thought to myself, *"okay come back to real time, you were just dreaming."*

Dreaming is something I do quite frequently when I'm in the outdoors. I dream of monster bucks and long-spurred gobblers while I'm hunting. I dream of 3-lb. crappie and 10-lb. bass when I'm fishing. As I read hunting magazines, I dream of being able to hunt in the places that seem to produce trophy deer year after year. I dream of owning more hunting land. I have dreams of many things that will probably never come true. There's nothing wrong with dreaming if it is kept in perspective. This kind of dreaming is completely controllable and is a choice.

Uncontrollable dreaming happens when we are asleep or semi-asleep. I surely have dreamed many things in my sleep that I would not have chosen to dream. Dreams can be scary and not make any sense at all. I don't know what causes these kinds of dreams, and I don't believe that every dream can be interpreted. I believe that some dreams are brought on by traumatic experiences and other things, but I also believe that eating too close to bedtime can cause weird dreams. I know that God sometimes speaks to us in dreams. The Bible gives us several examples of God speaking to people through dreams and visions. I believe with all my heart that God has spoken to me through dreams. Two examples of this are very clear in my mind and were so powerful that I'll never forget them.

It was July 4, 1980. My girlfriend, who is now my wife, was with me at my parents' house. We were celebrating the Fourth as we always did, with a fish fry and then a few fireworks. Back then, we would even fire off a few rounds with the shotgun just to make some noise. This became a ritual when I was younger. Back then, I would use any excuse just to shoot a gun. It wasn't unusual to hear gunshots in every direction. We filled our bellies with fried fish and frog legs and after it got dark, we began to set off a few fireworks, and I fired off a few rounds with my shotgun. It started getting late, so we stopped the noise out of respect for the neighbors and for Grandma who usually went to bed early. I took Johnsie, my girlfriend, home and returned to my house to go to bed.

When I woke up the next morning, I recalled a dream that I had been dreaming most of the night. It's rare for me to recall what I dream. This one seemed so real and clear. I remembered every detail. In the dream, my Granddaddy and Grandma were dancing. I don't mean slow dancing. They were kicking their heels up and having the best time. They were laughing and were just overjoyed about something. I began to wonder why in the world I had dreamed that. My Granddaddy had died exactly six months earlier and had been in poor health for most of my life. I certainly had never seen him or Grandma dance. Grandma was a very reserved, quiet person and probably the most influential person in my life. She was the rock foundation for our whole family. I remember tears rolling down my face as I visualized Granddaddy being so happy in my dream. I missed him so much. Grandma missed him so much that her smile was replaced with a longing solemn look. I had been worried about her and couldn't wait to go tell her about my dream. I was heading into the kitchen to tell my Mama and Daddy about it when my uncle who lived behind Grandma came to our door. He told us that he couldn't get Grandma to come to the door. She always rose out of the bed very early, so we knew that something was wrong. We soon learned that Grandma had passed away peacefully overnight in her sleep. So many emotions and thoughts were engulfing me. I couldn't breathe. The most important person in my life was gone. How could I go on? I was hurting so bad. Then I began to replay over and over, in my mind, the dream I had the night before. I knew, as I sobbed uncontrollably, that God had sent me that dream to tell me that Grandma was now with Granddaddy and that they both were dancing with joy. I knew that they were in heaven together. God knew how bad I was going to hurt and He sent me this vision, this dream, whatever you want to call it, to comfort me and help minimize my grief. According to the coroner, Grandma passed away during the time that we were celebrating with fireworks. How fitting. It was Grandma's going home celebration.

On another occasion, a few years later, I had something happen that I still don't fully understand and probably won't until I get to heaven and all things are revealed. My wife and kids had gone somewhere, and I had an opportunity for some quiet time and I decided to take a midday nap on the living room couch. I locked the doors. Anyone that knows me well knows that I'm not afraid of anything much in the world, but I am skeptical about being in my house alone. Although I'm prepared if it ever does happen, I've always had a fear of someone coming in my house uninvited. So, with doors locked, I settled in for what I hoped would be a long, restful nap. I'm not sure how long I had been asleep when I heard what sounded like someone walking around in the living room. I then became fully awake. There was no doubt that there was someone in the room with me. I tried to open my eyes, but they would not open. It was as if my eyelids were glued together. I tried and tried but could not open my eyes. I could almost feel the presence of someone very near to me. This was not a dream. I was awake. What is amazing to me is that I was not in a panic. I was trying to open my eyes to see who was there, but I wasn't afraid. I was at peace with whatever was going on. I simply could not open my eyes. After a few minutes, my eyes opened, and I jumped up and went through the house to find my wife and kids. I assumed that it was them that I had heard. There was nobody home. I began to tremble and wonder just who in the heck had been inside my house with me.

About that time, I looked outside, and my Daddy was pulling into my driveway. It wasn't unusual for Daddy to stop by, so I didn't think much of it. I went outside debating whether or not I should tell him about what had just happened. He said, "what are you doing?" I told him that I had just got up from a nap. He said "you ain't gonna believe what just happened to me." I could tell that he was shaken, and he looked as white as a sheet, so I asked him if he was alright. He said, "I was taking a nap in my chair out in the shop and my Daddy came to see me." Now Granddaddy had been in heaven for several years by then. Daddy's voice was quivering when he said, "for the first time in my life, Daddy told me that he loved me and that he was alright." My grand-daddy was a tough man who believed in hard work and that most everything else was foolishness. Daddy knew that Granddaddy loved him, but he needed to hear him say it. You can imagine the look on my Daddy's face when I told him that I thought Granddaddy had come to visit me too. That's the only explanation I have. I understand God sending Granddaddy, or a vision of him, to Daddy that day but I'm not sure why I had my experience. Perhaps it was just to give validity to Daddy's experience.

As for me, I believe that God still speaks to us through visions or dreams. We just need to listen for what He wants to tell us in them. I don't believe in dream inter-preters. I do believe that God has the answers when we wonder what dreams mean. I am so thankful for these two occasions when God surely spoke to and comforted me through these dream/vision/encounters.

Joel 2:28; Daniel 7:13–14; Numbers 12:6; Acts 2:17; 16:9; 18:9; Revelation 19:11–16.

⊰ 20 ⊱

Worth Imitating

Late July is when I begin to get the itch every year. It's usually too hot for fishing. I know that the bucks have been growing their annual racks for about three months and I'm always interested to see the potential wall hangers, freaks, and fawn crop. I usually start supplement feeding in my food plots with corn. I put out trail cameras. I've been feeding minerals all spring and summer. Bow season will be here in about six weeks and I'm excited.

Such was the situation in late July 2009. My cameras had been out for about a week, and I couldn't stand the anticipation any longer. I went to retrieve the SD cards out of the two cameras I had placed at two of my food plots. As I began to look at the pictures on my laptop back at the house, I was excited to see that I had some very nice bucks coming along. Their velvet covered antlers made them look bigger than they actually were, and it got my heart pumping. But what really caught my eye was a fawn. This particular fawn had only one ear. I had pictures of it every day. It was always by itself. I wasn't sure if it was orphaned or whether its mama just didn't come in to the corn pile. There appeared to be a nub left of the ear on its right side, so I don't think it was born that way. My suspicion is that a coyote attacked it and the fawn was able to get away minus one of its ears. Perhaps the coyotes caught the fawn's mama while she was trying to protect it. I'll never know the answers to those questions. I named the fawn "One Ear" and looked for it every time I checked my trail cameras for the rest of the year. It was always by itself, and soon after it lost its spots, I didn't get any more pictures of it. I was afraid that something had happened to it. I didn't even know if it was a buck or doe fawn.

I didn't get any pictures of One Ear all the following year, so I assumed that it had succumbed to disease or predation or possibly had been hit by a car. However, the following summer, in 2011, One Ear showed back up with two fawns of her own. She was a frequent visitor to the same food plot where I first got pictures of her as a fawn. I vowed that I would never shoot her and asked the neighbors to spare her also. Each year, I would get a few pictures of her with fawns and she always seemed to have twin bucks. By the time hunting season arrived each year, she would disappear, and I wouldn't get any pictures of her. I never saw her while hunting. This cycle repeated for eight years. I couldn't believe that she had lived that long. During the hunting season of 2018, when One Ear was nine years old, she stepped out into the food plot while I was hunting. Two button head bucks, her offspring for that year, and two spikes, which I assumed were her offspring from the year before came in to the food plot and began to feed. They kept looking back toward the woods from where they had come. I could see movement back in the woods and finally One Ear stepped out into the food plot. She would take a couple of steps then throw her head up to check the wind. She would look right up into the tree stand at me as if to say, "I know you're up there." She never fed on the clover or the corn. She walked up to the corn pile where her offspring were eating and took her front paws and smacked all four of them in the butt. She began to walk away and all four of them followed her back into the woods and I never saw any of them the rest of the season.

In the summer of 2019, I decided to put out some corn at the edge of my yard and put up a trail camera to see what I could get pictures of. It was amazing to see all of the creatures that came into my yard at night. I began to see several deer early in the morning and late in the evening coming to the corn pile. There were several fawns and does and a couple of small bucks that looked like twins. They soon began to come into the yard at all times of day. They would graze in my yard and then eat corn. One afternoon just before dark, there were several deer at the corn. I was watching from my bedroom window and all of a sudden One Ear stepped out. She was very cautious but went to the corn and began to feed. She soon became a common and frequent visitor to my yard. She only had one fawn with her that year. It was so entertaining to watch her with the rest of the herd. She was queen, there's no doubt about that. She would discipline the other deer that I assumed were mostly her offspring. All of the other deer would watch her and imitate whatever she did. She was their protector. She was full of wisdom from being around for such a long time. I imagine that her encounter, as a fawn, with whatever got her ear, made her other senses keener and made her both smart and cautious. I spent a lot of time watching her and the other deer trying to learn more about their habits, what days they did and what days they didn't feed. I tried to line that up with moon phases, the weather, and other things so that I could apply those things to my hunting strategies. I learned so much from watching her. What impressed me the most was how the other deer imitated every move One Ear made. When she decided it was time to go, they all left. When she decided it was okay to walk almost up to my porch, they all followed her, but they would never do that without her.

I began to understand that One Ear had probably saved the lives of other deer, especially fawns, many times. They all somehow knew that she was worthy of imitating. This got me to thinking about my offspring, my children and my grandchildren. Was I worthy of imitating? If they imitated me, what would they be imitating? This really hit me hard. These were hard questions and I needed to answer them. I knew that my grandchildren mimicked me whenever they were around me. They looked up to me, I guess because of my age and because I was their Papa. I was supposed to be the spiritual leader, guide, and protector in the home, and I began to wonder if I had done a good job of that when my children were still at home. I know they imitated me at times. I know that my wife looked to me for guidance and had imitated me.

The Apostle Paul said in 1 Corinthians 11:1 "Imitate me just as I also imitate Christ." This has become my favorite verse of Scripture and a verse that I am challenged by every day. Paul was not boasting here. He was saying, humbly, that he follows the example of Christ and that others should do likewise. In other words, Paul was in a position that I should be in and desire to be in. I should be living the example of Christ so that if anyone would imitate me, they would be following the example of Christ also. I surely want for those in my family that look to me to be the spiritual leader to be able to imitate me and by doing so, imitate Christ.

I believe that the entire deer herd on my property is stronger and smarter because of the life of One Ear. It is so because when her offspring imitated her, they were imitating what was best. It's interesting to me that One Ear became a leader worth imitating even though she was orphaned and didn't have an adult in her life to imitate. That should be a great hope for those who don't have godly examples as parents or grandparents.

It's really everyone's choice whether or not to be worthy of imitating. If anyone imitates you, will they be imitating what is best? Will they be imitating Christ? Will those you leave behind when you go home be stronger in Christ because of the life that you lived? One Ear was hit by a car in November 2019 at the age of ten and half. Her legacy lives on and her oldest doe offspring that is still alive has taken her place in the herd. I feel so blessed to have witnessed her life. Not many deer live to be more than three or four in the wild.

1 Corinthians 11:1.

I Got My Story

It was the second morning of muzzleloader or black powder season as some like to call it. I was in the tree well before light. I had been in the stand for about fifteen minutes when I heard the unmistakable sound of a deer walking in the leaves. It was heading toward my food plot. My heart began to race as it always does. The deer stepped out into the food plot and even in the dim light, I could tell that it was a nice buck. He was feeding on corn and clover and was oblivious to my presence aloft only 30 yards away. I glanced down at my phone to see what time it was. It was exactly ten minutes before legal shooting light. I was hoping that he would stick around for ten more minutes. I eased my muzzleloader up and looked at him through the scope. I almost came unglued at that point. It was the big 10-pointer that I had been after all of bow season. I had many pictures of him all summer and watched as he grew a beautiful, heavy rack. I had one picture of him after he shed his velvet then he vanished from the face of the earth, it seemed. With eight minutes left before legal shooting light, the buck of my dreams walked out of my life and back into the thick forest. I began to think, *"I sure hope this doesn't haunt me for the rest of the season."* I knew I had ethically done the right thing but it sure wasn't easy.

The next morning, I received a text from a friend across the road who said he had just shot the big 10. All sorts of things came to mind. I was thinking that I should have shot him the morning before and I said under my breath, "Well you had your chance, Dummy." But a voice in my head just kept saying, *"you did the right thing, and you will be blessed for it."* I sure had my doubts at that moment though. Then I received another text from my friend saying that he couldn't find any evidence that he had hit the deer and that apparently, he had missed. While I felt really bad for him, I have to admit, his misfortune did renew my hope.

On the morning of the last day of muzzleloader season, I woke up at 4:00 A.M. to get ready for another sit in the deer stand. It had been an unproductive season thus far with very few sightings of deer at all and only the predawn sighting of the big 10 throughout bow and muzzleloader season. As I was getting a dose of caffeine to bring me to life, I began to think about what God may be trying to teach me through this hunting season, this season of life.

Here is the post that I shared on social media:

As I head out this morning for the last day of muzzleloader season, I know that in all probability, today will be like the entire season thus far. The big one is somewhere else. The weather is horrible, the wind changes every 10 minutes, dadadadadada. My hopes are still high however that God will give me another story in life, another chapter for the book. You see, it was Him that gave me this passion as a gift to be used for His glory. Without that, I'm just sitting in camouflage, disgusted that I'm not successful by the world's standards, hoping for something that doesn't really exist. Lord, give me a story, a chapter to share. Fuel my passion with revelation.

As I was sitting in the stand that morning and again that afternoon, I began to think that I surely was right about today being like the rest of the season. I didn't see anything all day. I was wondering if God was going to give me a story, a chapter for the book. So far not much was coming to me in the way of revelation except that I seemed to be wasting time by sitting in this tree. Then I began to think about what I had said in my post that morning, particularly about how God gave me this passion to be used for His glory. I began to think about my grandson Levi and how he had, after several years of being disinterested, become excited about hunting again. He had killed a nice 8-pointer the first day of muzzleloader season and was planning to hunt with me the following day, which was the first day of gun season. It sure made me happy to see him excited about hunting again. Levi was fifteen-years-old and at a very impressionable age and I knew that this was an opportunity for me to spend time with him while living my passion. I wanted him to learn about hunting from me but, more importantly, to learn how to honor God while doing something that you are passionate about, whether you're being successful or not. So, there it was. God surely gave me a revelation. He revealed to me that Levi was going to be watching how I reacted on the good days and the bad days of hunting. He also revealed to me that all of my grandchildren were watching how I reacted on the good and bad days of life. So how could I share this and make it a chapter in the book? I had to wait another day to find out.

The following afternoon, Levi and I took our scent free showers, donned our camo, and sprayed down with scent eliminating spray. We checked to make sure we had everything we needed and talked about our hunting plan. I would be going to a stand that I've always called "the buddy stand." It was a 2-man ladder stand that had been very good to me over the years. Due to wind direction, I told Levi that I thought he should hunt the stand at what we've always called "the pea patch." I planted peas there many years ago and the name just stuck. That has also been a productive stand over the years with many kids taking their first deer there. I told

Levi to choose which stand he wanted to hunt. He chose the pea patch. I told Levi that the big 10-pointer was still alive because my friend across the road had missed him during muzzleloader season. I had pictures of him a few nights earlier on my trail camera at the pea patch. So, that was our hope: to get a chance at the big 10. We prayed and headed our separate ways. The last thing we always talk about is safety. I always say, "no deer is worth getting hurt over." As we both walked in different directions across the yard, we looked at each other and gave a thumbs up.

After sitting in the stand for a while, my phone vibrated, and I had a text message from my friend across the road. It said this, "the big 10 is dead." My heart immediately fell into my stomach. I texted my wife Johnsie and told her that the big 10 was dead. She knew how hard I had hunted for him and how bad I wanted him. My friend had not missed after all. He found the big 10 dead after seeing buzzards circling. This is something that no hunter wants to happen. There was no blood to be found or no indication of a hit the morning that my friend shot him. If you hunt long enough things like this will happen. Even though my friend was happy to find the big 10, he was also very upset. He had experienced several highs and lows over the last few days. He thought he had missed the big 10, then a big 9-pointer offered him a shot. He discovered that he had missed the 9-pointer. Then he found the big 10. Now that is an emotional roller coaster. We were sending texts back and forth when I realized that I had a trail camera picture of the big 10 the night after my friend shot at him. Now we were both really puzzled. Something just wasn't adding up. My friend said, "I don't know what's going on, I'm baffled."

I was really feeling dejected. I remember thinking that if my target buck was dead, what was the point? I began to pray, "Lord, I'm really feeling down right now. Could you please, if it can possibly be in Your will, send Levi something big?" Two hours later as the afternoon was giving up its fight to darkness, a shot rang out from the pea patch. I looked at my phone and it was exactly eight minutes until the end of legal shooting light. I knew that Levi would only shoot at a really nice buck or a coyote, so I immediately got down from my stand and, with my heart racing, walked/ran back to the house. Levi was already there and, as I was walking across the yard, I could see him talking and gesturing to my wife through the kitchen window. I could tell he was excited, and I was out of breath and about to hyperventilate. When I went in, he said "Papa, it's a monster and I know I hit him. I found blood then I ran back to the house."

Then my wife Johnsie told me that Levi had come in and said, "I shot the big 10." She told Levi that the big 10 was dead. Levi then said "I don't know, Papa. He's a 10-pointer and he's big, that's all I know." Then I calmed down a tiny bit and told Levi to share the story with me. I wanted to know where he entered the pea patch, which way he ran after the shot, whether or not he had heard the deer crash. I was asking all sorts of questions. Johnsie told me to calm down or I was going to have a heart attack. Levi said that he felt like he had made a good shot. I told him that we would wait a few minutes and then go start the tracking job. I was concerned about coyotes finding him before we did.

We went back over to the pea patch with flashlights and found the blood trail. We followed it about 20 yards into the woods when Levi said, 'Papa, there he is." The deer was bedded down about 20 yards from us but was still alive. He was moving his head around and all I could see was antlers. I could tell he was a very nice buck. He was in thick brush so there was no chance at a follow up shot to finish him off. Thankfully, I didn't panic. I whispered to Levi and told him that we were going to back out and give him some time to expire. I knew that if he stayed bedded when we were that close, he was mortally wounded. We went back to the house and Levi called his parents and I called my son Shane to tell them what was going on. I, honestly, was having an anxiety attack. I was pacing back and forth, wondering how long we should wait. I called my friend Randy Dunkley who is my taxidermist and asked him his opinion. I knew that there were three different packs of coyotes in the neighborhood, and I was so worried that they would either find him or jump him up and push him off my property. I described the situation and what the blood looked like to Randy. I told him that there was some bright blood but that some of the blood was dark and it looked like a liver shot to me. He told me to wait an hour and that Levi's deer would be laying there dead. I can't explain how long that hour seemed. I was a total wreck.

An hour on the dot and we were headed back to the pea patch. We slowly walked up on the buck and thankfully he had expired. Levi was in shock when he saw how big the rack was. Levi's Papa was too. This was the big 10 that I had on camera. This was the big 10 that I had been after all season. This was a different big 10 than my friend had shot. Now, it was all beginning to make sense. Who knew there were two big 10s? They looked really similar, so we had just assumed that there was one big 10 and he was crossing back and forth across the road. The truth is that I didn't have any pictures of the deer that my friend killed, and he didn't have any pictures of the deer that Levi killed.

God sure gave me the story that I had prayed for and I am so thankful to be able to add it as a chapter in this book. God knew all along that there were two big 10s, and He also knew that it would mean so much more to me for Levi to be able to harvest him than for me to. I thought that God had given me a story to share about when He says "no," but instead He gave me a story to share about when He says, "My child, I have something better in store for you." You see, Levi's big 10 was really THE big 10. It was the bigger of the two. Nothing to boast about, but just affirmation that God really does know what's best. Levi's deer green scored 142-7/8 and netted 135-2/8. That's bigger than any deer I've ever taken in my fifty years of hunting whitetails. I sure am glad that I did the right thing that morning. God doesn't always reward us right away—or even at all, here on earth—for doing the right thing, but He sure blessed me beyond measure in just a few days.

Jeremiah 29:11.

WONDER WHY?

My wife Johnsie asked, "are you going hunting this afternoon?" My reply was "no, the wind is going to be rough." Her classic response was "wonder why the wind is blowing?" She is always full of *wonder whys* when it comes to anything from why it is raining so much to why things cost so much. I've told her many times that she should write a book and title it *Wonder Why?* I think, if we are honest with ourselves, we all wonder why about many things that occur in life, especially bad things that sometimes happen to what we consider to be good people.

The Bible gives us many answers to the why questions and many reasons for things that happen. However, we can't always get definite answers or answers that satisfy us. That's when we must have faith in this truth in Romans 8:28, "And we know that all things work together for good to those who love God, to those who are the called according to His purpose". For Christians, this verse alone should be enough to satisfy our questions.

We should know that there are times when we are not going to have full understanding about what is going on in our lives and in the world. If we knew all the plans that God has for us and the answers to all of the questions, we would be equal to Him in knowledge. Why is it that God withholds answers to some of our questions? Perhaps, sometimes, it's simply that we don't ask Him to reveal answers to us or to give us understanding. I know I'm guilty of being full of questions but rarely do I truly seek understanding. We need to get on our knees and ask God for understanding and revelation in answer to our questions. Many times, He will supply those things through His Word if we would just stay in it, study it, pray about it, and dwell on it. I also believe that the all-knowing, perfect God knows what we can handle and how we would react if we knew all the answers. He knows best. That should be enough for those of us who call Him Father and say that we have faith and trust Him. Having said that, I realize that we all are human, and we want answers. My prayer is that God will forgive me when I don't trust Him enough to give me what He knows is best and to withhold from me what He knows is best.

Being joyful in all things is not an easy task or attitude to have. Many times, I've wondered why it couldn't be in His will for me to kill a big buck or why His will for me right now was that I don't have time to hunt or fish. But much more important than things such as this, I wonder why such bad things are allowed to happen.

Why do people kill one another? Why does God allow people in authority who push things like abortion and make laws that go against the sanctity of marriage? Why does God allow the ungodly to govern? I have so many questions that I won't get satisfying answers to until all things are revealed in heaven. Nevertheless, I get anxious about these things. I worry about these things and sometimes even live in fear over these things. God has told me not to worry, to be anxious, or to be afraid. He's got it.

There have been times in my life when I needed answers to tough questions. Questions such as "why does my Daddy have to die so young with a brain tumor?" Another one was "Lord, why are you making my sweet Mama suffer so bad when she has been such a faithful servant?" God hasn't fully answered those questions for me yet, but He has given me a certain amount of understanding.

After my Daddy had brain surgery and was somewhat reduced back to childhood, he told me one day that he was ready, as a matter of fact, he kept saying it over and over. He would say "I'm ready, that's what matters, I'm ready that's what matters." Now that is a peace for me that is beyond all understanding. I know that he was ready and that truly is all that matters. I know that these few years that I've had to live without him will be replaced with an eternity with him.

My Mama was dying in the hospital and there was absolutely nothing they could do for her. Due to lack of blood flow, her intestines, for lack of better wording, died. She had emphysema and struggled to breathe. During the last few days, I was sitting out in the lobby. They would only allow me to be in the ICU with Mama for a certain amount of time. A young man came into the area and was talking on the phone. I could tell that he was very upset. He got off the phone and I spoke to him. He started talking about his Mama who had been in ICU but was now in a regular room. He was upset at his siblings because it seemed that he was having to do everything for his Mama. His siblings weren't there with him and he felt like he had no help. I told him that I understood because I was the only child and I felt like I had to do everything myself too. He asked who I was there for. I told him about Mama. He went on to tell me about his Mama and was still very agitated at everything that was taking place. He told me that his Mama was going home the next day. Then he asked me when my Mama was going home. I said this "my Mama won't be going home; they are only giving her a day or two to live." His demeanor immediately changed, and he started saying that he was sorry. I'll never forget what he said next. He said, "how can you deal with that?" Then he said, "I really feel bad complaining about my situation, at least I will be able to take my Mama home." There was the open door, I began to witness to him. I truly have no idea exactly what I said to him and I had no intentions of witnessing to him, honestly. I just began to say what God gave me to say. I basically told him that my Mama was going home too but to her eternal home and that I was good with that. I told him that I would miss her but that I knew I would see her again. I wasn't expecting what happened next. That young man got down on his knees and began to weep. I'm not sure if that young man accepted Christ into his life or not that day but I do know that a seed was planted. Looking back, I wish I had gotten his full name so that I could have followed up with him. One thing is for sure: I'll know one day what the fruit of that seed was. I had no idea what I was doing. It was all in God's plan. Was that the answer to the question, "why are you making my Mama suffer?" Knowing my Mama, she would have gone through everything she went through gladly, if it meant that someone she didn't even know would come to Christ. That's the kind of special, loving lady she was. A soul meant that much to my Mama and it means that much to our Father. I look at it this way, God gave me two of the greatest blessings I've ever had in the midst of the two most tragic things that have ever happened to me. What an amazing God.

As I was wondering about many things one day, God gave me a song. It's probably one of the simplest songs I've ever written, and it took the least time to write. It became one of the most requested songs that we performed when we had our Christian contemporary band, "Stumble No More." It was the first song that we recorded in the studio for our CD and it was my Mama's favorite song. She told me that she had many favorites but "I Know Jesus" was her favorite song of all time and that she wanted it played at her funeral. We were able to play the recorded version of the song for Mama during her last hour as all of her loved ones gathered around. Her body was failing quickly, but her mind and her heart were 100%. We played it again at her funeral, and there was not a dry eye in the church. My daughter Anna's beautiful voice echoed through the church with a hope that was so comforting. Oh, what a special day it was, seven years later, when her four great granddaughters Emmie, Alayna, Ellie, and Alyvia, sang it in church while my son Shane played the guitar. Below are the lyrics.

I Know Jesus

Why do God's people suffer?
Why is there so much pain?
I don't know, I just don't know.
Why is it those who have everything, feel the need
to complain?
I don't know, I just don't know.

But I know peace
And I know joy
I know God's grace and love and mercy
And so much more
And I know Jesus, I know Jesus, I know Jesus.

Why do little babies have to die?
Why do we have to fight?
I don't know, I just don't know.
Why is it things that used to be wrong, all of a sudden
are right?
I don't know, I just don't know.
But I know peace
And I know joy
I know God's grace and love and mercy
And so much more
And I know Jesus, I know Jesus, I know Jesus.

I can't answer all the questions.
I don't know everything.
But if you ask me what I do know,
This is what I'll sing.

I know peace
And I know joy
I know God's grace and love and mercy
And so much more
And I know Jesus, I know Jesus, I know Jesus,
I know Jesus, I know Jesus, I know Jesus.

Johnsie is still full of the wonder why questions, but we both know that what really matters is that we know Jesus. That's really all that matters.

Romans 5:3–5; 8:18, 28; James 1:2–3; John 9:1–41; 16:33; I Corinthians 13:12, 13; Isaiah 57:1; Psalm 10:1–18; Luke 18:19.

23

NO FEAR

A long bearded thunderchicken (AKA) gobbler was showing up almost every morning in my clover patch. That's what the trail camera images revealed. He loved to strut right in the middle of the half-acre field that I had planted just for him and his buddies. It was almost turkey season and I knew that there wasn't a tree on the edge of the clover field big enough for me to set up against and try to get him. I ordered a portable blind and hoped that it would be delivered in time for the opening morning of turkey season. I had never hunted from a portable blind before but was excited about trying it. It sure worked for the turkey hunters on TV.

The delivery truck arrived with the blind on Friday around noon. I knew that I had to hurry and get it set up and brushed in quickly because the next morning was the first morning of turkey season. I got the blind set up and brushed in, and I had high hopes for the morning hunt. I checked to make sure that the camouflage, shoot through netting on the windows of the blind would conceal me from that old gobblers' eyes. I couldn't see through the camo netting from the outside so I was confident that if he came in, I could make a move and shoot him without spooking him.

I was in the blind well before light the next morning. My plan was to stay silent and not do any owl hooting and no calling in hopes that the gobbler would follow the same pattern that he had been following every morning. As dawn approached, I heard a gobble on the other side of a big field on my neighbor's property. I wasn't sure if that was the gobbler that had been coming to my clover patch or not, but it was the only gobble I heard so I assumed that it was. My thoughts were that he probably wouldn't bypass that huge field to strut in and come over to my small field. After a few minutes I heard him gobble in the big field and knew he was getting closer. He kept coming closer and a hen flew down and landed right in front of my blind. I was very thankful for that camo window netting. The hen never knew I was there. The gobbler was on an old logging road that led to my clover patch and was coming fast. The hen, thankfully, didn't go to him but remained in the clover patch pecking away at the clover. Soon I saw the red, blue, and white head of that magnificent bird. He was in full strut right in front of my trail camera. I let him strut around for a few minutes so I could get some good pictures of him. He was gobbling, strutting, and drumming and I couldn't take it any longer. My 3-1/2," 12-gauge Mossberg shotgun put the smack down on him and about knocked me out of my chair that I was sitting in. Getting that zipper unzipped on the blind was a challenge with all my excitement. I ran over to him and he was flopping all over the place but wasn't going anywhere. He had long spurs and a long beard and was a really big bird. I was so happy that my plan had worked, and I felt like a real turkey hunter.

I retrieved the SD card out of my camera, grabbed that big ole thunderchicken and headed to the house just as proud as a peacock. After my wife took some pictures of me with the bird, I plucked and cleaned him. That breast was going to be mighty delicious. I shoved the SD card into my laptop and was anxious to see the hunt captured in pictures. I had to go through several days of deer, squirrels, birds, possums, and raccoons to get to the morning of the hunt. I started scrolling through the pictures for that date and at about 5:30 A.M. that morning, my camera captured what I thought at first couldn't be real. It was a huge black bear. Now, in my part of the world, there are very few black bears and I have never actually laid eyes on one except in a zoo. Keep in mind that my trail camera was only about 20 yards from the blind that I was hunting out of. I had several pictures of the bear. He actually laid down at one point and was licking the minerals that I had put out for the deer. I was so excited to have a bear on camera. I started sending the pictures to my wife, daughter, and son. Then it hit me like a ton of bricks. That bear was 20 yards from my portable blind as I walked in for my turkey hunt that morning. I guess it ran off when it heard me and saw the light from my flashlight. The thought of that made me tremble a little. I am very unfamiliar with bears and I know that if I had to wrestle one, I wouldn't fare so well.

That got me to thinking that if I had known that bear was there, I surely wouldn't have gone and got in that blind in the dark that morning. I would have been afraid to. Why would I have been afraid? There are many reasons, but the main ones are that the bear was much bigger than me and I was so unfamiliar with bears and didn't know what the potential was. Anyone who knows me knows that I'm not afraid of very much in this life, except for yellow jackets; they terrify me and will make me hurt myself to get away from them. But I think that fear of the unknown would have prevented me from going turkey hunting that morning if I had known the situation. Fear would have caused me to miss the blessing of that hunt and the beauty of that majestic bird strutting around.

I believe that fear causes us to miss many blessings that God has in store for us. Because we are afraid of the unknown or afraid that something is much bigger than what we can handle, we miss out on opportunities to do what God has set aside for us to do. God surely will get His will accomplished, whether we are the instrument or not, but when He calls us to something, He desires for us to get the blessing from answering the call. Fear, many times prevents us from accomplishing the work that God has called us to do, therefore we miss the blessing. God has given us 365 examples in His Word that say, "do not fear" or "do not be afraid," yet we still live in fear. I used to believe that God gave us one example to encourage us not to fear for every day of the year. I no longer believe that. I believe that He gave us 365 examples of do not fear or don't be afraid for every day of the year. Some days we may need all 365.

Psalm 23:4; 27:1; Isaiah 41:13; Luke 14:27; Deuteronomy 3:22; Matthew 10:28.

⊰ 24 ⊱

ARE YOU THE WINNER?

I t was January 2, the first day after deer season is closed every year. When weather permits, I always spend this day hiking in the woods. For the first time since turkey season ended in mid-May, I wasn't worried about spooking deer. I didn't have to be quiet. I wasn't afraid of getting busted by a big buck. I didn't take a scent free shower. Why was I hiking in the woods? I was looking for rubs, old scrapes, paths and bedding areas that might give me clues on where and how to hunt that elusive monster buck the following season. Sadly, it's also a time to look for carcasses of deer that may have succumbed to disease or predation or even another hunter's poorly placed shot. I keep my eyes open also for things like box turtle shells, old shed antlers, Native American artifacts, unique rocks, feathers, and anything that nature has provided that is interesting.

It was on one of these days that God gave me the revelation for this story. I was hiking along the creek that runs through my property. I had been up and down the rolling hills that make up the terrain in my neck of the woods for several hours. I was carrying a backpack filled with bottled water and snacks, a folding saw, matches, and old toilet paper rolls for starting a campfire, if I so desired, and of course toilet paper should it be needed. I looked at my health app on my phone and it indicated that I had walked about 8 miles that day, zigging back and forth through the woods and in the creek. Those hills and my age had left me winded and tired. I decided to sit for a while on a massive old oak tree that had fallen during a windstorm. I began to think back about twenty years to a time when I was walking at least 8 miles every day in preparation for a Relay for Life event.

It all began when my parents started walking every day at a local park as part of a mid-life health kick. They invited my wife and I to join them one day, and we all went and walked around the track for about thirty minutes. We really enjoyed it, so it quickly became a ritual for us all to go and walk every evening. My wife and I began to walk longer and further, and we had worked up to 3–5 miles every day. Soon, that was not enough for me. I began to push myself to walk more miles and to walk faster every day. Understand that God designed me to be an all-or-nothing person. When I do something, I give it my all or I'm not going to do it at all. Whether or not that is always a good trait is debatable.

At about the same time that I was becoming obsessed with walking, the campaign began for the annual Relay for Life event in our county to raise money for cancer research. Part of the event involved walking around the track as a team or individual. The idea was to raise money on the promise of walking in the event as an individual or as part of a team. I had a coworker who was battling cancer at the time, so I had the idea to try and raise money in her honor and walk as part of my team from work. I began to think that it would be a great way to raise money if I would do something out of the ordinary. I decided to raise money on the promise that I would walk 50 miles in the relay. I have no earthly idea where the 50-mile number came from. The only thing I can think of is that my daddy used to tell me about doing 50-mile forced marches in the army and how tough it was. I started getting sponsors and began to train every day by walking anywhere from 5–10 miles. I really pushed myself and quickly realized that walking 50 miles was going to be a tough promise to keep. A couple of my coworkers came on board with me and promised to try and walk the distance with me. Donations were coming in daily and people were excited to see me attempt this walk. I think most of them had in their minds that there was no way that I could accomplish this but were supportive of my effort to try.

The day finally came for the 1997 Relay for Life event and, although the main event started in the evening, I along with my two coworkers began to walk very early that morning. Around and around that track we walked. All day we walked. Blisters formed on my feet.

We stopped only briefly for a snack or a bathroom visit. We walked and we walked. There was nowhere on my body that wasn't hurting. Evening came and the event began. We kept walking. Others were now walking with their teams. Most walking only a few laps at best. Out of respect, we stopped walking long enough for the cancer survivors to take their lap around the track. Then it became emotional. Tears began to flow as I saw my coworker and others that I knew walking that track. Some had defeated cancer, and some would lose their battle to it. I had about ten more miles to go and physically, I didn't know if I could do it. My feet were bleeding, my legs were cramping, my back was hurting, I was about dehydrated, and I wanted to stop. That's when God picked me up and carried me. The last 10 miles were a complete blur. People were encouraging me and asking if I needed anything. Right then, all I needed was for God to keep carrying me on His shoulders. I pressed on until the last lap. My wife held me up and half toted me on the last lap. I honestly don't remember much after that. I know we went home, and I collapsed on the bed.

The following morning, we got up and I hobbled to the shower. We had to go back to the track for the closing ceremonies. I wasn't expecting what happened at the ceremony. They called my name as the top fundraising individual and I had to go up to accept a plaque. I had raised over $3,000 and I had to give an acceptance speech. I was totally unprepared for that. I remember thanking everyone for their support and thanking my two coworkers Ronnie and John for walking with me. I talked about my coworker Betsy, who was fighting for her life, and how courageous she was. I thanked God for getting me through the walk but that's about all I had to say about Him.

I truly don't remember whether I walked in the relay in 1998 or not. I know I was on a team from work and a team from my church and worked to raise money for the event. In 1999, I decided to make a 50-mile walk again. My wife Johnsie and several others from my church decided to walk with me. So that it wouldn't be so monotonous, we decided to walk 25 miles out on the highway in the country and 25 miles around the track. So, I mapped out a 12.5 mile route out in the country. The plan was to start at the track, walk 12.5 miles out and 12.5 miles back to the track, then walk the remaining 25 miles around the track. We began early that morning and returned to the track about mid-afternoon. We had all stayed together for the first 25 miles but now everyone was on their own. Some, like me, rested for a little while and some kept walking—wanting to get it over with. Again, it was a grueling task. I know that we all were physically worn to a frazzle. I do recall that Johnsie lost a toenail and decided that this would be her first and last 50-mile walk. I don't recall how much money we raised that year, but I know that our county was the top fundraising county, for our size, in the country. As a church team, we prayed before we began the walk and thanked Him afterward. Looking back, I think we had an overlooked opportunity for great testimony for what God had allowed us to accomplish.

During the next year, Cathy, a dear friend and one of the church members who walked the 50 miles with me, was diagnosed with cancer and the prognosis was not very good. For the 2000 relay, I pledged to walk 50 miles once again, in her honor. I began to train for the event and to raise money. Cathy was an amazing lady, and the donations began to pour in. I was a member of three different teams that year: a team from work, from the gym, and from my church. It was highly advertised that I would be attempting the 50 miles in Cathy's honor and a reporter from one of the major newspapers in our area called and set up an interview with Cathy and me. Cathy was a very humble person and didn't want all this attention. Honestly, I didn't either but we both agreed that we would do the interview in hopes that it would bring attention to the cause. I remember the reporter asking Cathy her thoughts on all of this and her response was "I am just so truly thankful." I don't think the reporter was prepared for that from a lady who was basically dying from cancer. The lady reporter began to cry and so did I. Cathy just smiled. My thoughts at that moment were that I had never seen a more beautiful lady or soul than I was sitting beside right then. I made the 50-mile walk at the event and wanted to do something extra for Cathy so I walked 30 additional miles for a total of 80 miles. Again, I was the top fundraising individual for the event. I raised over $15,000 dollars for cancer research in honor of my friend Cathy Garrett. In my acceptance speech, I honored Cathy, thanked our sponsors, cried, and thanked God. I also think that I began to notice a pattern. It seemed as if every year, I was winning some kind of award for raising money and walking the most miles of anyone. My friend Cathy went to be with her Lord later that year. I can't wait to see her again one day.

What motivated me the following year to do something even bigger, even better? I don't know. Was it pride? Was it self-worship? Was it the fact that my friend had passed away with cancer and I'd had two more friends who had just been diagnosed? Was it truly for the cause? I dare say, a little of all of those things were what possessed me to dedicate myself to walking 100 miles in the upcoming 2001 relay. I started my walk on Thursday morning and walked all day and all night Thursday night. They left the track lights on for me. EMS came over twice and bandaged my swollen feet to help with blisters. The only other company I had all night was a skunk that walked several laps around the track following me. That gave me a little motivation to move faster. I walked all day Friday while the teams were setting up for the evening event. The high school kids, including my son and daughter, were cheering me on. My daughter came down and walked a few laps with me and some of my friends did also. The event started and there were so many people cheering for me and encouraging me. I finished the 100 miles about midnight that night after all of the festivities were over. There were people camped out around the track but most of them had gone to sleep. Again, Johnsie was holding on to me and helping me the last few laps. At the closing ceremonies the following morning, I hobbled up to the stage barefooted to receive my award for raising the most money again. Again, I thanked all the sponsors and everyone who supported me and thanked God for getting me through it all. Another missed opportunity to testify.

As best as I can remember, I took a break from walking in the 2002 relay but was on a team that raised money for the event. Up to this point, I had never had a family member with cancer. In June of 2003, my Daddy was diagnosed with incurable brain cancer. There are many testimonies I could share about this chapter in my life. The 2003 relay was all about rolling Daddy around the track in a wheelchair for the survivor's lap. Daddy succumbed to brain cancer just after Christmas that year.

In 2004, we formed a family relay team in memory of Daddy. I remember my daughter Anna making Christmas tree ornaments from seashells to sell for our fundraising efforts. And yes, I decided, much to the dismay of my wife and Mama to walk 100 miles in memory of Daddy. The past year had taken its toll on all of us emotionally, mentally, spiritually, and physically. I just wanted to do something special for Daddy. I began my walk on Thursday morning like I had in 2001. I had not trained hard enough. I wasn't physically prepared, and my feet were not calloused. I was depending on emotion and guts to get me through this. I walked all day Thursday and into the night on Thursday night. It was about midnight and I was all alone at the track. Johnsie had gone home to get some sleep so she could work the next day. I stopped to take a break and eat a snack. I sat down on the ground. I took my shoes off and my socks were soaked in blood. I wrung them out and put my shoes back on. I had walked 43 miles. I had a long way to go. At that moment, I began to think about Daddy and started sobbing uncontrollably. I could vividly hear him saying to me something that he had said before my 100 mile walk in 2001. He said, "Son, you don't have to prove anything to anybody." I began to wonder what I was trying to prove. I began to think back on all the walks I had made and wondered why I had truly made those walks. When I tried to get up, I fell. I called Johnsie and told her to come and get me. She asked if I had finished. I simply said, "it's over." I could not physically or emotionally walk another mile or another lap, not even another step.

The next day, as our family team was setting up for the evening's events, I felt like I had let everyone down. I felt like I had let Daddy down. I felt like a failure. Family members kept reassuring me, encouraging me, and crying with me. At the luminary ceremony that night, we had hundreds of luminaries in memory of Daddy and we had an entire set of bleachers reserved with luminary bags with his name on them. As we lit them, his words came back to me again, "Son, you don't have to prove anything to anybody." The next morning, at the closing ceremonies, I was shocked when they called me up to accept the award for raising the most money. I had no idea and didn't have a speech prepared. In total humility, this time I got it right. All the walks, all of the blisters and blood, the cramps, the aches, the mental and emotional anguish over the years came down to a time of testimony. As tears flowed, I testified to God's greatness. I told the crowd that no matter how much we walked or how much money we raised, nothing was going to change until we got on our knees and prayed that God would intervene. Then, totally unrehearsed, I began to pray. I prayed for those who had, and were currently, battling cancer. I prayed for all the care givers. I prayed that God would use all of the hard work that had been put in at these events to His glory. I prayed for doctors and nurses. I prayed for a cure if it was in His will. I prayed that God would take the ugliness of cancer and make good come from it. I thanked Him for sending His son to save us so that no cancer or any other disease could defeat us. I don't think there were many dry eyes there that day.

I've never walked in the relay since that day but have supported it. The last time I went, I made one lap around the track and ate something at about every one of the booths. God revealed much to me through the years of walking. One of the greatest things He revealed to me was this: It has nothing to do with who is best, who is first, who has the most points or runs. It has nothing to do with who goes the furthest. It has everything to do with who glorifies God in the midst of the endeavor. For that one will surely be declared the winner.

With renewed strength, I grabbed a snack out of my backpack and headed up the hill to check out a good location to put a deer stand for the next season, all the while wondering how I could honor God even in this.

> Isaiah 40:31; 1 Corinthians 10:31; Colossians 3:17.

✥ 25 ✥

BE COMMITTED

I had my cane pole, a can of worms that I had dug up near the spring in the pasture, and a long piece of twine to secure any fish that I might catch. It was a very simple way to fish but the only way I knew how to. I was at my granddaddy's pond. I was about ten years old and I had never caught anything bigger than a hand sized bluegill. I had been fishing for a few minutes and so far, had only managed to drown some worms. Then I caught a small bream. I had the idea to put the small bream on the hook and fish with it. Maybe I could catch a bass or a big snapping turtle. Darkness was coming quickly, and I had another idea. I was going to leave my cane pole overnight with the tiny bream on it to see if a big bass would come along and devour the smaller fish. I would check first thing the next morning to see if I had caught anything. I laid the pole down and put a rock on top of it. I thought that the rock would keep anything from pulling the pole in the pond.

I was excited to get to the pond the next morning and got up out of bed very early. This wasn't anything unusual for a young boy who grew up on a tobacco farm. I told Mama and Daddy that I would be back in a few minutes and I ran all the way to the pond. When I got there, I realized that my pole was gone. Something had snatched it out from under the rock. I looked out into the water and saw my pole floating near the far side bank. I ran over to that side and the pole began to move. Something was pulling it across the water and was going out into the middle of the pond. As fast as it was moving, I imagined a fish as long as my leg was attached to the hook. I followed that cane pole around and around the pond. Every time I would get near it, it would take off again. I was so excited. I remember saying "God, if you will just let me catch this fish, I'll do whatever you want me to for the rest of my life." After a few minutes, I was able to grab hold of the cane pole. I had a fight on my hands and finally landed a beautiful bass. I thought it was the biggest bass in the whole world. I found out later that it weighed just over 5 lbs. It was the biggest fish that had ever been caught out of granddaddy's pond and I remember him being about as excited as I was. In days to come, I began to think about the commitment I had made to God that day. How in the world was I going to keep that commitment? Of course, I have broken that promise many times in my life. In fact, a commitment like that is impossible to keep. Thank God for giving us a way to make amends with Him when we don't keep our commitments to Him. As a little boy, I didn't quite understand about making good on commitments or forgiveness. As an adult, I understand the seriousness of commitment and the immeasurable greatness of God's forgiveness.

Staying committed to something is never easy. I'd like to have a nickel for every time I've started an exercise routine or a special healthy diet. I stay committed for a time but always falter. I decided to make a commitment a few years ago to only shoot mature bucks off of my property. I realized that if I shot nice two and one-half-year-old bucks, they would never reach their potential. Keeping that commitment has been very difficult. When a buck steps out that gets your heart pumping, it's hard to take the time to evaluate whether or not he is mature. While I have been disciplined enough to let good young bucks walk over the past few years, I've folded under the excitement on a few occasions and shot bucks that I wished later I had given a pass.

One of the biggest commitments that we can make in life is marriage. Marriage is a commitment that, sadly, is taken about as lightly these days as the commitment I made to God as a little boy if He would let me catch that fish. God has much to say about marriage and the sanctity of it. I had a friend who was getting married several years ago and I began to think about my wedding day. I wrote part of this song for that occasion and then added to it when two of my special friends in Alaska were to be married to each other. Here are the lyrics.

When I Say I Do

On this special day we'll stand
As a woman and a man
Expressing our love for all the world to see
With a promise to each other
That we will love one another
For the rest of our lives unconditionally.

When I say I do, I really do
For the first time in my life I know
This love is really true.
No more running around and searching
Always wondering who.
When I say I do, I really do.

I don't know what life is gonna bring,
But with you my heart will always sing
When I say I do, I really do.

When I say I will, I surely will.
No more climbing up, stumbling
Then rolling down that hill.
I've finally made it to the top
And now I'm standing still.
When I say I will, I surely will.

I don't know what life is gonna bring
But with you my heart will always sing.

When I say I will, I surely will.
I'm so in love with you.

I've made so many mistakes over the years when it comes to my marriage commitment. Realizing when you're not living up to your end of the deal is the first step in getting back on track and staying committed. As I'm writing this, my wife Johnsie and I have been married for thirty-eight years. A couple of years ago, on our anniversary, someone asked me what the secret was to a long, healthy marriage. I'm certainly no expert on that subject but it got me to thinking about what has made our marriage so good and what it has taken for our marriage to be successful. I came up with a list that is certainly not a complete list but a fairly good list, I believe, for any marriage.

(1) Always put God first, period. He comes before your spouse and your children, before your dreams, your desires, your career, before everything.

(2) Respect and honor one another with your words, even when you want to strangle each other. Don't speak harshly about one another or one another's family.

(3) Look in the mirror, not in vanity but in self-check mode. Walk away, then go back and look again before you face your spouse. If you're good looking, it's okay to look a third time.

(4) Don't holler at each other. The kids will think it's normal and start doing the same thing. Unless, like me and Johnsie, you are hard of hearing. Then it's perfectly acceptable.

(5) Agree to disagree. It's not a victory to always be right. You never learn or grow unless you're wrong. Be willing to admit when you are.

(6) Never make your spouse feel like they have to compete for you. Make them feel like they are the winner and you are the prize.

(7) Compliment, compliment, compliment.

(8) Encourage, encourage, encourage.

(9) Forgive, forgive, forgive.

(10) Don't separate anything. You're in this together. The money is y'all's not yours. The property is y'all's not yours. The children are y'all's not yours.

(11) Stay off social media when you are together and be together.

(12) Remember your vows; live them.

(13) Understand that the grass on the other side of the fence is greener because there is fresh cow poop there.

(14) Listen and hear.

(15) Make eye contact and discover over and over why you married this beautiful person.

(16) Remember that spouses are people too and they make mistakes just like you do.

(17) Never talk negatively about your spouse to anyone, not even your spouse.

(18) Laugh, laugh, laugh, mostly at yourself.

(19) Love, love, love, with everything that you have inside you, with your heart. Love others before yourself. Others includes your spouse. Tell your spouse, (say it, say it, live it, live it), that you love them.

(20) Put God first in all that you say to them and all that you do with them, for them, and away from them.

(21) Put God first.

The greatest commitment that any of us can ever make is the commitment to follow Jesus. It is a commitment that we will struggle with daily. It is a commitment that like all other commitments requires a great measure of discipline. It is a commitment that is impossible to keep 100% of the time. I'm so thankful that God forgives us when we falter and don't keep that commitment. As with marriage, we could probably come up with a long list of things that would help us stay committed in our walk with the Lord. A very short list would be to stay in His Word, stay on your knees in prayer, seek knowledge and revelation from Him, and be willing whenever He calls you to something. I desire one day for people, but mostly God, to say "he fought the good fight." Oh yeah, like me that day as a little boy, don't make deals with God that you know you can't keep. God is not in the deal-making business, but if you accept Him, He's ready to make the commitment to you that He will give you eternal life with Him.

> 2 Timothy 4:7; I Kings 8:61;
> Proverbs 16:3; Psalm 37:5.

ATTENTION TO DETAIL

E very hunting season starts off the same. A week prior to the opening day of bow season, I start thinking about scent control and elimination. I instruct my wife Johnsie to start using my scent eliminating laundry detergent so that all of the good smelling, deer deterring detergent can be flushed out of the washing machine. The day before the first hunt, I wash all of my hunting clothes, even my underwear, socks, towels, and bath cloths in the scent eliminating detergent. I wash my hands with scent eliminating soap before I take the clothes out of the washing machine and put them into the dryer. I use scent eliminating dryer sheets. I wash my hands, once again, with scent eliminating soap before I remove the clothes from the dryer. Then I take them outside and put them in my scent eliminating, carbon filtered, scent free duffle bag.

The first thing I do before deciding which of my stands to hunt on a particular day is to look at the weather to see what the wind direction is forecasted to be. I am very cautious about accessing my stand and want to make sure that the wind won't be blowing toward where I think the deer are bedding. I also don't want the wind to be blowing toward where I expect to possibly get a shot. If the wind is wrong, I simply don't hunt that stand that day. Being retired gives me that option now. I've always got tomorrow to hunt if the Lord allows me to wake up. Prior to each hunt, I take a shower with the scent eliminating soap and dry off with, yep, the towels that I had washed in scent eliminating detergent. I don't touch anything in the house that could possibly put human scent on my hands. I go outside, naked as a jaybird, and begin to put on my hunting clothes. I can do the naked as a jaybird thing because nobody can possibly see me except the birds and squirrels. After I put my clothes on, I spray down with scent eliminating field spray. I then put my scent eliminating, knee high, rubber hunting boots on. I either put camo makeup on my face or wear a camo mask so that my face won't stick out like a light bulb in the middle of the foliage and camouflage that I'm wearing. I look in the mirror to make sure I look like a tree and then grab my bow. The last thing I do before walking to the stand is to get down on one knee and pray. I walk very slowly, being cautious not to step on any leaves or sticks, all the way to my stand. I approach the stand as easy as I can and begin to climb the ladder, being careful not to make any noise at all. While I'm in the stand, I'm as still as the guard at the tomb of the unknown soldier. A mosquito can take a chunk out of my ear and I'll just sit there and take it. Movement has ruined more deer hunts than any other single thing, in my opinion. I tell my family not to text me unless it's an emergency, but I have my phone in case there should ever be one. I move my eyes from side to side, and not my head, to cover the area that I'm watching for deer movement. I guess you could say that I'm a scent free freak and extremely particular about every detail.

As the hunting season progresses, especially after the bow and muzzleloader seasons have ended, I tend to let my guard down a bit. I begin to think that the best hunting is over for the year and start taking shortcuts. I don't worry as much about wind direction because I just want to hunt. I may wear my hunting clothes for a couple of weeks without washing them again. Sometimes, I don't wear a face covering or even apply camo makeup. I don't worry as much about spooking deer as I'm walking to my stand and I'm not as cautious about my steps. I can usually be found looking at my phone for much of the hunt and I move around more. I haven't been very successful over the years with late season hunts, and I usually attribute it to the fact that most of the nice bucks have been killed or they have become nocturnal. While this is definitely true, I believe that much of my lack of success is due to inattention to detail. I can only imagine how many deer have winded me or seen me during late season hunts and disappeared without me ever knowing they were there.

I've witnessed this same scenario with people in the workplace. Typically, people tend to put their best foot forward when they first get hired. They may be very particular about doing the very best they can to do a good job. I've seen it over and over, however, that after working at the same job for a period of time, some people tend to slack off a bit in their attention to detail in their work duties. It's only natural I suppose, but it can have negative consequences. Great evaluations and pay raises may turn into bad evaluations or average evaluations without pay raises and advancement. Slacking off could even lead to layoffs or termination.

The missed opportunity at a nice buck or the possibility of being terminated from a job are not pleasant to think about but pale in comparison to the result of inattention to detail, or no longer being particular, in our spiritual walk. I've experienced this in my own life, and I don't believe that I'm the only Christian who has slacked off after being a Christian for a while. When we first get saved, we tend to be on fire for the Lord. We make sure that we go to church, we read our Bible, we want to be involved in mission work, and volunteer to help wherever needed. At least this was my testimony. As the years go by, sometimes we get comfortable in the assurance that we are saved and nobody can take that away from us. We may have grown in Christ for years but now it just seems like we know enough about Him. Maybe we feel as if we have served on enough committees at church or been on enough mission trips.

Perhaps we have read God's Word through many times and we know what it says and don't think that we need to study it anymore or seek revelation from it anymore. This kind of thinking by Christians can be devastating to our spiritual lives. God desires for us to keep seeking, keep working, and keep sharing. Without attention to detail in all of these things, we can end up down in the valley when we were once on top of the mountain. There is much work to do and God has a plan for us to be involved in that work until we take our last breath. He didn't create us or save us to be idle. I believe that when we are on top of the mountain, there can be a tendency for us to have a bit of self-worship and when we are down in the valley, it's hard for God to use us. Speaking for me, I think that God uses me when I'm still climbing and reaching for the top of the mountain. Every step is a struggle, but God has gotten me this far. My goal is to keep climbing so that I reach the summit with the last breath that I take. On a hike up a mountain in Alaska, with a torn cartilage in my knee, God gave me these words and I sang them loudly. Only my fellow missionaries and the bear and moose heard me. The bear and moose ran off and the missionaries just shook their heads.

I've been up on the mountain
I've been down in the valley below,
Right now I'm somewhere in the middle
Searching for which way to go.

Lord, show me Your face, in this place,
Send me blessings that can't be erased.
I just wanna know, I just wanna know
Which way to go.

It's mid-December and here in North Carolina that means that deer season is coming to an end in three weeks. It's late season, but I'm about to go wash all my hunting clothes and check the weather for wind direction.

Romans 12:1–2; Colossians 3:17; Psalm 32:8.

⊰ 27 ⊱

GET BACK ON THAT HORSE

———————————————

Hunting has its depressing days—days that make you just want to quit. Every hunter who hunts long enough will experience this. Sometimes it's due to missing an animal. Sometimes it's due to wounding an animal and not recovering it. Sometimes, it's simply due to sitting in a stand day after day without seeing anything, or at least anything that you consider to be a shooter. I've come home from all three of these scenarios with head hanging, complaining that I never have any good fortune, the wind and weather were against me, and a dozen other complaints. I know that Johnsie grows tired of this every turkey and deer season. She always has something positive to say. She'll say, "I'm sorry, maybe you can get one tomorrow," or something along those lines. I'm so thankful that she doesn't say "suck it up" or "I wish you would just "shut up" or perhaps "stop being a big baby." Her positivity helps to keep me going. I always do suck it up and go right back the next day and try again. Sometimes it seems as if I'm a sucker for punishment, but the truth is that I know that if I drown in my sorrows, I'll never kill a trophy buck or a big gobbler. So, I do what I've always heard, and I get back on that horse when I fall off. Growing up on a farm helped me to understand the ups and downs of doing anything that is worth doing. The biggest buck I've ever taken was three days after I had missed a 10-point giant with my bow. The biggest bass I've ever caught, an 11-lb. 2 oz. beauty, was in my bucket only minutes after I had lost another big one when it spit out the hook.

My granddaughter Alayna gave me a great example to follow when it comes to getting back on the horse one Sunday morning. Alayna was nine years old and had just recently accepted Christ as her Savior and was baptized. Her and all of my other granddaughters had been singing at church almost every Sunday for several months and Alayna had sung a few solos. She called me on the phone one night and said "Papa, I wrote a song." I put the phone on speaker, and she sang her song for me and Johnsie. I was overcome with emotion and quite surprised at how structured and good this song was. Being a songwriter of sorts myself, I am very critical of music and original songs, but I really liked this one. The very next Sunday Alayna decided to sing her song at church with my son Shane playing the guitar for her. I was all set to video her performance. She was very nervous. When she began to sing, I thought *"man, she is sounding so good."* Then she just stopped singing. She had begun the second line of her song with the wrong word and she realized it immediately. I almost panicked. I felt so bad for her and I thought that it was over. I expected her to be so upset that she would just stop for good and walk off the stage. My son Shane kept playing. Then Alayna started her song over again and absolutely nailed it. Her performance brought the house down, or should I say, she brought God's house down. She did such an amazing job. I was so proud of her for many reasons. I was proud that she wrote this song all by herself. I was proud that she sang it beautifully. I was proud that she had the courage to stand up there and perform it. But most of all, I was proud that when she faltered, she didn't quit. When I posted her video on social media, I didn't edit out the part when she messed up because that was the most teachable moment and the moment when me and God were proudest of her.

One of the best examples of not giving up, in my life, happened on mission in Alaska. Our team had been to Alaska four years in a row on mission in a large park. Our mission was to supply lunch, do crafts, have Bible study, and play and just love kids. Our mission became much more than that and soon we were helping families with needs, ministering to homeless teenagers and adults, assisting those who had addictions to find help, and sharing the love of Jesus to the people of Alaska. It seemed as if, after four years, we had not made any progress as far as people coming to know Christ or accepting Him as their Savior. After all, that was the ultimate goal. I began to wonder if our mission was working or if we were making any difference at all. The following summer we were told that we would be going to a different park that was in a neighborhood. It was a small park that only had a few kids coming to it. When we arrived at the park for the first time, I was devastated. We had been serving in a huge park with a playground, tennis and basketball courts, skateboard park and all sorts of things for kids to do. This new park had one little piece of playground equipment and a few painted tires for the kids to play on. I thought to myself, *"Lord, did you really send us 4,000 miles for this?"* We started our park ministry and only had a handful of kids the first day. The next day there were a few more and some adults. By the end of the week, we had about twenty kids and adults coming every day. God allowed me to lead three kids to Christ and my heart was completely overwhelmed and overflowing.

The following summer, we requested the same small park in Palmer, Alaska. We had begun relationships that we wanted to nurture and couldn't wait to get back. I also had a burdened heart about the kids who had accepted Christ the summer before. They had not been baptized when they'd accepted Christ the past year, so I started asking if that was possible and after I was told that we could baptize them at the park, I began to work on getting parental permission and talked with each one of the kids to see if they wanted to be baptized. All three really wanted to so I sat them down and explained all about baptism. We were to baptize them at our evening park party in a horse trough filled with water right there in the park. We invited the whole community. The day of the park party, God allowed me to lead two more kids to Christ, so I got permissions to baptize them also. That night was absolutely amazing. I had wanted so badly to baptize these kids myself such as Philip baptized the Eunuch. When I had asked originally about the baptism, I was told that one of the local pastors would be performing the baptism. The morning before the baptism, I was told that something suddenly came up and the pastor couldn't be there. I was asked by Jay, the GraceWorks staff member, if I would like to perform the baptisms. I was overcome with emotion. That night, I baptized five kids at the park. It was incredible how God was working in this little park. I now could see why God sent us to this tiny park. After four years of no visible fruit in the huge park, we now were seeing fruit in abundance in this most unlikely place. I began to realize that it took all those years of being obedient and sharing the love of Christ to get to this point. If we had hung our heads after four years or even refused to work in such a small park that seemed to be a lost cause, none of this would have transpired. The third year in the Palmer park, two more kids came to know Christ and I was blessed to baptize one of them. At our final circle prayer in the tiny park on our last day before we had to fly back home, we had sixty-seven kids and adults holding hands and praying together. When I shared the picture with the head man for GraceWorks, Scott Kirby, he was simply amazed. He said that the first year they tried to have the ministry in the tiny Palmer park, the leader of the mission team came back and told him that it would never work. They only had three or four kids coming every day and he thought that it was a waste of time, money, and effort to continue the ministry there. I'm not judging that pastor. My initial thoughts were exactly the same but I'm so thankful that our team didn't give up and we got back on that horse for seven years. Below are the lyrics to Alayna's song.

On the Cross

I have heard this old, old story
And I'm sure that you have too.
It's about our Lord and Savior
And He died for me and you.

On the cross, on the cross
He died for us on the cross;
On the cross, on the cross
He died for us on the cross.

I have heard this old, old story
And I'm sure that you have too.
It's about our Lord and Savior
And He died for me and you.

On the cross, on the cross
He died for us on the cross.
On the cross, on the cross
He died for us on the cross.

I am here to tell you this story
It's about our Lord and Christ.
He died for us and our sins
Well isn't He so nice?

On the cross, on the cross
He died for us on the cross.
On the cross, on the cross
He died for us on the cross
Yes, He died for us on the cross.
Oh, He died for us on the cross.

Galatians 6:9; Luke 1:37; Matthew 19:26.

28

SOMEWHERE OVER THE RAINBOW

I could hear it thundering off in the distance. With every boom from the sky, a double gobble came from one of my food plots. I suppose that's where the name thunderchicken came from. I was standing on my back porch wondering if I had time to go after him before the storm hit. I ran in the house and threw my camouflage on, grabbed my gun, and headed toward him at a fast pace. I knew this was going to either happen quick or I was going to get soaking wet from rain. The forecast was for potential severe storms. In the spring, in north central North Carolina you never know what the weather holds.

I got as close as I dared to the fired-up gobbler and set up beside an oak tree. I started sweet-talking him with my diaphragm call. He gobbled every time I yelped and every time it thundered which seemed to be more often every minute. That storm was coming fast. The problem was the gobbler wasn't coming fast. Actually, he wasn't coming at all. He was just teasing me from the center of the field. I was within 100 yards of him and he was making my heart beat out of my chest with every gobble. Suddenly, a streak of lightning lit up the sky followed by an immediate crack of thunder. I was on my feet and running back to the house about as fast as a middle-aged, fat man can run. It began to hail as big as nickels. It was coming down so hard that it sounded like it was tearing the trees down. I was completely out of breath and exhausted when I reached my back porch. Lightning struck close by and I surely was glad to be back home. I went inside to dry off and get out of the storm. It was a quick storm but did a lot of damage around our county. There was hail damage, wind damage, and a house got struck by lightning and caught on fire.

When the storm went by, I went back outside on the porch. I was pretty bummed out because the storm had messed up my hunt. Then I looked up into the sky at the most awesome double rainbow that I think I've ever seen. It was so clear and had all the colors that a rainbow should have. I began to think back to my childhood to a day when my sweet Mama told me what rainbows mean and what they stand for.

It must have been a Saturday because me and Mama were home and Daddy was working. I was about five years old. We lived in a single wide trailer back then on the family farm. A storm much like the one I described above, was approaching. That was back before we had all of the warning devices that we have now for bad weather. The only warning we had was a black sky to the southwest with the sounds of thunder and the wind had started blowing fiercely. As most everyone knows, a single wide trailer is not the place to be in a bad storm, so Mama grabbed me by the hand and half drug me to the car. I didn't want to go outside because I was scared. She told me that we would be safe in the car. I remember so vividly that I was terrified as the wind began to rock our car and the lightning and thunder were coming only seconds apart. It was my first experience with hail. I thought it was going to bust the windshield out. I was crying and Mama was trying to calm me down. She began to tell me the story of the rainbow. The things I remember about what she said have always stayed with me through all of the storms of life. Remember that Mama was talking to a small child. She told me that God promised Noah after the flood that He would never destroy the earth by flood again. She said that the rainbow is a sign of God's glory and His faithfulness. Of course, I was full of questions. She had me really interested to the point that I had forgotten all about the car rocking and the hail hitting the windows. She said that the rainbow was a promise from God that He would protect us from the devil and that He was always near and would comfort us. Those things that were true and from God's Word comforted me. In fact, my Mama's words that day have comforted me many times in my life. A simple, true promise from God spoken in words that I could understand as a child had a tremendous impact on me that stormy day and even today. The storm finally subsided and right on cue God put a magnificent rainbow in the sky. It seemed as if it was placed right over top of our little trailer.

On another occasion in Hatcher Pass, Alaska, God reminded me of His faithfulness and promises once again. I, along with several of my friends/missionaries were climbing up to the summit at Hatcher Pass in the pouring rain. Our goal was to climb to the top so that I could do one pushup. Yep, one pushup. It would be the one millionth pushup that I had completed since I had left Alaska exactly one year prior. The pushup story will be in another chapter of this book. What I want to portray here is a year long, grueling calling from God coming to a much-anticipated fruition. Certainly, I had not anticipated that it would be raining cats and dogs. There would be no time during our week-long mission trip to come back to Hatcher Pass, so I had to get this done now if I was going to accomplish this task the way I had envisioned it. We all wrapped up as best as we could—with me, of course, forgetting to pack my raincoat—and proceeded up to the summit. It was raining so hard and we all were soaked to the bone. Keep in mind that this is a fairly steep, tough climb. We all pushed ahead and made it to the top. I was going to do my pushup and then head right back down. Then just as I was about to do my pushup, the rain stopped, and the most beautiful close arch rainbow appeared. Everybody was taking pictures and in awe. It had been so foggy all the way up to the top that we could hardly see a few feet ahead of us but now it was clear. It was as if the sky opened up, the rainbow appeared and God said, "I told you I would be faithful to you if you heeded the call." Now, if I ever had a sign that I was exactly where God wanted me to be doing exactly what He wanted me to do, that moment was it. He had promised me that He would be with me during this impossible task and that He would see it through to the finish. It gives me chills every time I go back and look at those pictures and recall that day.

No doubt about it, the rainbow is a sign, a symbol of God and godly things. I'm very saddened by the fact that, in today's world the rainbow is being used as a symbol, by some, of sin. It has been used in such a gross manner that when I personally see a rainbow in the hallway of a school, I wonder what the motives are. The rainbow is God's. It is not ours and it surely isn't to be used as a symbol of anything other than what God has promised.

That thunderchicken should have never been so vocal during that April storm that day. He revealed his location and that was a mistake on his part. I harvested him about a week later and as the sunlight shone on his beautiful, colorful feathers, I was reminded once again of the rainbow.

Genesis 9:9–14; 15–17; Ezekiel 1:26–28; Revelation 4:1–4.

29

GOOD RIDDANCE

We were having our traditional Sunday night supper at our house. Our children and grand-children were all there. When we all get together, I honestly can't hear myself think. The kids are playing and there are usually about three different conversations going on with the adults. Total chaos and it's loud. It was one of those Sunday nights when I was so glad they all came but breathed a sigh of relief when they left. I had just undergone knee surgery two days earlier and was walking on crutches. My knee was wrapped up, swollen, and felt like it weighed a ton. As soon as they all were gone, Johnsie and I went to bed. I was worn out.

About five minutes after we got into bed, we heard what sounded like dishes being clanged together. The sound came from the living room. Johnsie got up to investigate and noticed that some of the decorative plates that she had placed on top of our mantle for the fireplace had fallen. Keep in mind that Johnsie is a short little beauty and very petite. She placed her hands on top of the mantle and got on her tip toes in order to reach the plates. That's when I heard a blood curdling scream and she yelled "snake!" When her head had cleared the top of the mantle, a 5-foot-long black snake was staring her right in the face. I fell out of bed and got to my feet, grabbed my crutches and proceeded to hobble into the living room. What happened next is something that I guess I'll never live down. Johnsie has forgiven me but I don't think she will ever forget it. The black snake was beginning to crawl down the side of the fireplace. I took one of my crutches and swung at it as hard as I could, trying to knock it down into the floor so that I could somehow kill it. Well, I missed the snake and hit Johnsie in the shin. So now she was yelling in pain. After I apologized, my focus went back to the snake. I finally got him in the floor and smashed his head with the bottom of my crutch. I threw the snake out in the yard and we cleaned up the blood that was all over the floor. There was absolutely no sleep to be had the rest of the night for us.

I know that some people think that I should have captured the snake somehow and released it unharmed. After all, black snakes are beneficial in killing mice and such. Here lies the debate of all debates. There are those who say things such as "the only good snake is a dead snake" or "kill 'em all" and things such as that. I don't feel that way at all. There are also those who consider you to be cruel and scum of the earth if you kill any snake. I don't feel that way either. I've been bitten on the hand by a Copperhead and struck on my boot three times. I let snakes live all the time in my yard and on my property. If a black snake is away from the house, he gets a pass. Copperheads, which I consider to be the prettiest snake that we have in my part of North Carolina, usually don't get a pass no matter where I encounter them even though they are my favorite snake. I like Copperheads because they hold their ground. They don't pursue you; they just don't tend to run away from you. I like that trait in people as well. Black snakes on the other hand will either chase you or run away from you. They are either too bold or they are cowards. These are traits that I don't like in snakes or people. But being as black snakes and all others in my neighborhood—except the Copperhead— are nonvenomous, I usually let them live and kill the venomous Copperheads. However, when any snake gets in my house or is trying to get in my house as was the case recently, they must go. I consider killing snakes like that good riddance.

The Bible has a lot to say about snakes or serpents. I will let you read the verses of Scripture and decide for yourself about snakes and their purpose. I do know that they are referenced several times when satan is on the scene. I know, that if God created them (and He did), that they have a purpose. Whether that purpose is good or evil, I'm not sure in all cases. I know that they serve a good purpose in that they eat insects and rodents, but they also eat turkey eggs from the nest and baby rabbits and such. I think a proper balance is the key just like it is with all creatures. I know that snakes were used by satan and cursed by God to crawl on their bellies. I also know that God gave us dominion over them and said that we would bruise their heads and they would bruise our heels. So, there will always be a love/hate relationship between snakes and people. God designed it that way.

From my perspective, there are times when snakes need to be gone from me and there are times when I need to look at the overall picture and decide whether the snake is more of a benefit or a hindrance. There are times when there are people in our lives who have become a hindrance or a stumbling block to our walk with the Lord. In other words, they are toxic. We need to remove those people from our lives. There are times when we need to look at the overall picture and continue to deal with people and give them the benefit of the doubt also. We would do well to look at the examples of David and Paul in the Scriptures and some tough decisions they had to make about removing people from their lives who were major barriers between them and getting God's work done. I'm all for giving a snake or a person a chance or several chances for that matter, but when a snake is threatening me or my family or a person is threatening my walk or my calling from God, they just simply have to go. Good riddance.

Samuel 26:17–25; Acts 15:36–41; John 8:58–59; Matthew 12:13–15; 23:33; Genesis 3:14–15; Revelation 12:9.

30

RESCUE III

I'm not sure exactly when it began. Although I was not necessarily seeking it, I began to receive revelation from God in the strangest places and at the strangest times. It wasn't while I was reading God's Word and it wasn't when I was praying or while I was at church. God began to speak to me and reveal things to me while I was sitting in a deer stand or while I was sitting on the bank by my pond fishing or even when I was walking in the woods. He spoke to me in a clear voice as I was walking on the beach looking for shark's teeth. He brought His Word home to me as I was trying to call in an elusive gobbler or even while I was sitting by a small fire by the creek as my ancestors did so many years ago. There is no doubt about it; God was speaking to me, but why? So much of what He has revealed to me never left the woods or the water for such a long time and much of it has been forgotten. I've noticed lately however, that He is jogging my memory and some of those forgotten revelations are coming back to me.

After dwelling on these God sent revelations for many moons, I began to consider that maybe God wanted me to share what He was giving me with others. I didn't really know exactly how to do that. I did take every opportunity that I had to share some of what He had revealed whenever I was talking with someone. Being a person who keeps to myself most of the time didn't allow for much of this sharing to take place, so I started sharing some on social media. Like anything from God, some welcomed what I was writing with open arms and asked for more, and some ignored it or lashed out at me for revealing God's truth. As odd as it may seem, both of these scenarios encouraged me and gave me fuel to keep it up. I knew that there were some who were being touched by what I was writing, and I also knew that some were being convicted and didn't want to hear it at all. I guess I felt somewhat like a preacher who steps on toes from the pulpit. I knew that I was in God's will at that point. As time went on, I felt a call from God to put all of these revelations in a book. I remember questioning God about this. I basically said "Lord, I don't even like to read. Are you sure you want me to write a book?" Like any call from God, it seemed ridiculous, impossible, and uncomfortable. That's how I knew that it was exactly what He wanted me to do. I wrestled with God about this for several years but never made any moves toward doing what He had asked me to do.

At some point during this time of disobedience, I started seeing the number 111 everywhere. It seemed that if I looked at my phone, it would always be 1:11 or 11:11. My posts on social media would say that there were 111 people who had reacted to them. I know that it seems strange, but I was seeing this 111 so much that it started to really annoy me. Like all of us usually do, instead of seeking an answer for it from God, I went to the internet and searched 111. I won't even share with you all of the weird things that came up, even satanic things. I began to get concerned that satan was messing with me. The 111 number was everywhere I looked, and it wasn't getting any better. I felt really stupid, but I told my wife, Johnsie about it and she started recognizing that 111 was showing up all over the place also. Typical Johnsie always said, "wonder why?" This went on for a long time before I did what I should have done in the beginning. I turned to God's Word and I asked God to reveal to me what the significance of this number was. It didn't take long at all, once I gave it God, to determine what it meant, I began to get answers. One of the first verses of Scripture that I looked at spoke to me so loudly that it has become the daily verse that I try to live by. It's 1 Corinthians 11:1 where the Apostle Paul says, "imitate me just as I also imitate Christ." I wrote about this verse in an earlier chapter. The challenge to me is to live every day of my life so that if others imitate me, they will also be imitating Christ. Was this it? Was this what God was trying to get through my thick skull by

RESCUE 111

having this number show up so much? I kept digging in the Scriptures and couldn't come up with anything else so I thought that this must be what God is trying to instill in me.

As time went on, I actually started writing the book that I had felt the call to write. I would call it *Deer Stand Revelations* or *Outdoor Revelations* or something of the sort. I was writing almost every day, chapter after chapter. I wrote about all the things that I could remember that God had revealed to me through the outdoors. I couldn't keep up because revelations were coming constantly. In the meantime, that 111 number didn't go away. In fact, it was getting worse and more frequent. It was almost as if God was saying "you still don't get it." I was thinking to myself, *"Lord, I do get it; I do understand and I'm trying to live my life as You would have me live it."* So, after 29 chapters were completed for the book and 111 showing up every day, I turned back to God's Word seeking something more. I couldn't be still. I couldn't sleep. I felt like there was something more that God was trying to tell me. I was writing but not with urgency. Then in the last book of the Bible, where I never would have dreamed of looking for an answer, God gave me this: Revelation 1:11, saying "I am the Alpha and Omega, the First and the Last," and "What you see, write in a book and send it to the seven churches which are Asia; to Ephesus, to Smyrna, to Pergamos, to Thyatira, to Sardis, to Philadelphia, and to Laodicea". Oh my goodness, this was it. This is what God had been trying to tell me all along. In essence, like John, God was telling me very clearly to write it in a book. I knew that God was calling me to this, but this really gives me affirmation. Also, like John, I know that my God inspired book won't be accepted or even acknowledged by many, but I also know that God wants me to write it because someone can benefit from it and it will ultimately somehow glorify Him.

So that's why it seems that this chapter is out of place. Chapter 30 at first glance seems as if it would have fit better as Chapter 1. But right in the middle of the book, God rescued me and gave me affirmation and a sense of urgency to complete the task that He has called me to.

Revelation 1:11; 1 Corinthians 11:1.

31

SIX MORE WEEKS

For so many years I was successful in limiting out on turkeys and deer. During this same time frame, it seemed that I was catching huge, trophy bass every year. It was a time of plenty when it came to the abundance of wildlife. I had a favorite fishing hole that produced every year. I had plenty of places to turkey and deer hunt. My son Shane was experiencing some of the best hunting and fishing that any little boy could dream of. I'm so thankful that he was successful at such an impressionable age. He got hooked early and still is an avid hunter and fisherman.

Then coyotes and disease came on the scene in our part of the country. North Carolina wildlife didn't know how to coexist with coyotes and were easy prey for a long time. Thankfully, it seems as if the coyotes have been here long enough that the deer and turkey population has wised up to them. A viral infection called E.H.D. disease wiped out many of the deer and the turkey population was on a drastic decline. Habitat decline and chemicals decimated the Bobwhite Quail. On top of all that, my favorite fishing hole was destroyed when the oxygen content suddenly dropped during an extreme temperature change in the water. Almost all of the fish died. It had taken years and years for the pond to become a trophy fishery. To add to these dilemmas, most of the private hunting land that used to be owned by farmers was now being leased out to the highest bidder for hunting at prices that the average guy couldn't afford.

This past year, I didn't even work a gobbler much less kill one. I only heard one gobble the entire season. I didn't kill any deer either. It was the same for Shane. I didn't have an opportunity at any buck that I would harvest, and I didn't shoot any does for meat because my herd is on the decline. I found three dead deer on my property that had succumbed to disease. All of this has made me realize that during the successful years, I wasn't as appreciative or thankful as I should have been. As I look at the trophy mounts of deer, bass, and turkeys in my home, I long for the days of abundance again. A lack of success over the last few years has made me so much more appreciative when I am successful and has made me realize that it is a true blessing to be able to harvest an animal or catch a big fish.

Last February 2, Groundhog Day, everyone was hoping that the groundhog wouldn't see his shadow so we would have an early spring. I was hoping that the groundhog would see his shadow and that we would have six more weeks of winter. When I shared that on social media, folks were calling me crazy. I wanted six more weeks of winter so that when spring finally arrived, I would truly appreciate it. In North Carolina we have spring teaser days all winter long, so when spring does arrive, we aren't as appreciative of it as we should be.

My thoughts go back to a time when I was a boy growing up on the family tobacco farm. The hottest days made us appreciate the cold water we drank from a mason jar at the end of the row. Hard knocks in life have made me appreciate the smallest things. I have no room for protest, for negativity, or for complaining because my heart overflows with thankfulness and joy. I am who I am, what I am, and where I am because of the winters that I have endured. God tells us to give thanks in all circumstances and rejoice always. I know that the next lunker bass I catch or the next deer or turkey that God allows me to harvest will be extra special and long overdue. I will surely give God the glory and thank Him for the opportunities that I have had to enjoy the bounty of His creation.

1 Thessalonians 5:16–18.

⚜ 32 ⚜

WELL, HE WARNED ME

M y daddy was small in stature but had the courage of a pit bull crossed with a lion. He was the Alaska featherweight state champion boxer in 1957 and 1958. Point being that he wasn't afraid of very much here on this earth except for dogs and game wardens. He had his share of run ins with the law before he found Jesus. He wasn't about to break any game laws. He respected all law enforcement, but it was just something about a game warden that terrified him.

I remember on one occasion when I was probably about twelve years old, when his fear of game wardens had an impact on me. We were deer hunting with hounds. Back in those days, there weren't many deer at all and running hounds was the only way anyone hunted deer in our neck of the woods. No one around here even knew how to still hunt for deer. Deer had been almost exterminated from our part of North Carolina and a restocking program had been introduced in the 1960's. We were hunting in the county where the stocking program was introduced, and a limited deer season had been established by the North Carolina Wildlife Resources Commission. I don't recall what the limit was on bucks, but it was illegal to shoot does. On this particular day my Daddy had told me that he would stand by me and support me on just about anything or any trouble that I got in to but that if I shot a doe deer, I was on my own. There it was. I had been warned.

We were standing under a power line and the dogs were coming. We could hear them in the distance. The sound of the hounds was exciting. I had never seen but a handful of deer much less shot one. I had only hunted squirrels and rabbits and had become a fairly decent shot on small game. The hounds were getting closer and closer. Daddy whispered to me, "don't shoot if it's a doe." About that time a small doe busted out of the woods and into the clear cut under the power line where we were. I remember so vividly Daddy yelling "don't shoot, don't shoot." Pow, the gun went off, the damage was done, the doe was down. I don't know if it was all the excitement or what that caused me to disobey my daddy. That wasn't something that I was accustomed to doing. I ran over to the dead doe. I was excited and scared and several other emotions. I turned around to see where Daddy was. I knew that I was going to be in trouble. When I turned to look toward where he had been standing, he wasn't there. As a matter of fact, I couldn't find him anywhere. Then I heard his truck crank up and leave. *What in the world?* Daddy had just left me. I don't know whether he was truly trying to teach me a lesson or whether he was so terrified of game wardens that he panicked. Whatever the case, he was gone, and I was there standing over an illegal deer all by myself. I was shocked and scared. I didn't know what I was going to do or how I was going to take care of this deer or even get home. Remember that there were no cell phones back then or even walkie talkies. At least we didn't have one. Thank goodness, one of my uncles had heard the shot and came to help me, and my cousin ended up driving me home later. I had thought that maybe Daddy was just teaching me a lesson and would be back to get me in a few minutes but that's not what happened. He drove the twenty miles back home and there he stayed.

When I got home, I was expecting a whipping but instead Daddy just looked at me and said, "I warned you what I would do if you ever shot a doe deer." There you go. He had been good to his word and his warning. There wasn't anything I could say to that. I actually gained much respect for my daddy that day and for game laws also. Hopefully, being almost fifty years ago, the statute of limitations applies and any game wardens reading this won't be knocking on my door.

God has given us many warnings as to what He will do if we disobey him and break His laws. The Bible is filled with warnings from God. Whenever we don't heed these warnings there are consequences. Being left alone by my daddy on that day was scary but being left alone by God, to live in our own iniquities, because we continue to disobey Him, is something I don't even like to think about. As a nation, I believe that we are almost at that point. It didn't take but one mess up for me to have a desire to follow and adhere to game laws for the rest of my life. I pray that there is a desire for our nation to turn back to God and follow and adhere to His laws before it is too late.

Ezekiel 3:20–21; 25:17; Proverbs 16:18; Romans 2:5; 6:23; John 3:36; 15:6; Isaiah 26:21; Matthew 10:28; Revelation 19:11–21; Hebrews 10:26–31.

33

An Encouraging Word

I t was the first morning of turkey season and I was in my blind well before dawn. I had made all of the necessary preparations. I had two hen decoys out in front of me as well as a jake decoy. I was hoping that the jake would make any gobbler that showed up mad enough to come in for a fight. At about 8:00 A.M. there was a gobbler behind me in the woods tearing it up. He was gobbling up and down the creek bottom. After about an hour of this it became fairly obvious that he wasn't going to come in to my setup.

It was one of those turkey hunting situations when you just don't know what to do. Should I move or should I stay put? Should I call more or get quiet for a while? After I had hit him hard with yelps, clucks, and purrs to no avail, I tried the silent treatment for a while. He just kept walking up and down the creek, gobbling at everything. I was getting impatient and knew that it was just a matter of time before he either got up with some hens or got disinterested. I decided to make a move and go after him. I secured my calls and gun and stood up. I was about to unzip the door on the blind when I heard a raspy yelp about 50 yards in front of me on a logging road. I couldn't see but about 20 yards in that direction, so I had not seen anything coming. I recognized the yelp as that of a jake. I sat back down and started talking back to him. Then there was a gobble. It was the kind of gobble that experience had taught me was a longbeard. The jake was yelping, the gobbler was gobbling, and then hens started cackling and purring. Then I saw that majestic red, white, and blue head and a gobbler strutted up to the decoys along with two jakes and three hens. I watched him for a few seconds and then I let my ole 12-gauge do its job. When I shot, the gobbler went down, and I jumped up. I heard a putt beside me and caught a glimpse of the gobbler that had been gobbling all morning running off. He had sneaked in to my setup after all.

The point of this story is that I was about to make a poor decision that would have messed up my hunt that day when that jake encouraged me with his terrible sounding, raspy yelp. Hearing that jake made me sit back down and gave me renewed hope. If I had unzipped the blind and stepped out, all of the turkeys would have been spooked and my hunt would have been ruined. Because of an encouraging word, or in this case a yelp, my perspective changed, and I ended up looking like a great turkey hunter.

An encouraging word from you or me, at just the right time, can change someone else's perspective and make their day. A word of encouragement could save someone's life or at least save them from making a terrible decision. On one occasion, in Alaska, God put me in the right place at the right time and gave me the words to say to a young lady who was contemplating ending her life. I honestly don't know exactly what I said to her. I do know that I told her that there was hope in Jesus no matter what her circumstances were and that He loved her. God used my tongue to say the words that He wanted to say to her at that moment. Timing is critical, but that's not ours. That is God's. We just need to be encouragers and be available for Him to use to encourage people wherever we go and whatever we're doing. We should be encouraging those who are lost so that they may be saved, and we need to encourage our brothers and sisters in Christ to stay the course. If you need an encouraging word and those around you just don't seem to be supplying it, go to God's Word. You can start with John 3:16.

> 1 Thessalonians 5:11; Hebrews 10:25;
> Proverbs 16:24; Ephesians 4:29.

⊰ 34 ⊱

WRONG SIDE OF THE FENCE

Spring on the farm meant a lot of different things when I was a young boy. One thing it meant every year, for sure, was that we would be getting up hay. We had square bales back then and every bale had to be lifted by hand and thrown up on a trailer. It was hot, itchy, hard work for anyone, much less for a young boy. My cousins and I had the job of loading the bales on the trailer while my uncle drove the tractor. He would drive along in the field very slowly and the expectation was that we would keep up so that he wouldn't have to stop the tractor. It was a challenge for three young boys and a competition also. None of us wanted to be the one who made our uncle have to stop the tractor.

It was on a day such as this that I learned a lesson that I am reminded of almost daily in my spiritual walk. We had loaded the trailer with hay bales several layers high to the point that we needed to go and unload it. We had stacked the bales as high as we could throw them, and the load was a bit unstable. Rather than walk from the hay field to the hay shed, I decided that I would ride up on top of the hay bales. The hay shed was inside of the cow pasture that had several cows and a bull in it. We raised cows to eat and to sell at the stock market. One of my cousins opened the gate to the pasture and my uncle made the turn with the tractor probably a little too fast. Did I mention that the load was a bit unstable? You guessed it. The load shifted, the hay came tumbling down and I came down with it. The fall was bad enough but where I landed was even worse. I just so happened to land right in the middle of the freshest cow patty in the whole pasture. I had cow poop from head to toe. Had I fallen off on the other side of the trailer, it would have hurt but there was no cow poop there. I can still hear my cousins laughing at me. Needless to say, I had to go home and do a bit of cleaning up. At least I got out of loading the hay back on the trailer, but I think it was worth it to my cousins to have to do it by themselves.

My mind goes back to that day often. What made me fall off on the wrong side as I was straddling the hay that day? I've had other occasions where I've fallen off on the wrong side. I've come to the conclusion that whenever I have made the mistake of "straddling the fence" as I like to call it; I've always fallen off on the wrong side. I've found that if you live life half on and half off, eventually you are going to be completely off. My experience has shown me that off is never a good thing. A dangerous proposition at best, fence straddling can be painful. It has caused me much pain and hard knocks in my life. Not to mention that barbed wire is not very forgiving.

God has much to say about straddling the fence. God warned us what He would do if we were lukewarm; neither cold nor hot. A doubleminded man cannot expect to receive anything from the Lord. We can't serve Him and serve the world at the same time. If we live like that, we will always end up serving the world. We can't have two masters. The question that I had to ask myself was, "Do I want God to be my master or the world?" In essence (no pun intended), do we want to be riding on a stable load or do we want to end up in cow poop?

Revelation 3:15–16; James 1:5–8; Psalm 119:113; Matthew 6:24.

35

BUCK FEVER

I never know when it's going to happen or how to stop it from happening. Sometimes a doe triggers it; sometimes a small buck, triggers it. Almost always a sizeable buck brings it on and sometimes just the anticipation that something might step out causes it. My knees shake violently and at times, my whole body. My mind starts racing with thoughts of "you've got to calm down" or "why in the world are you going crazy over a doe?" It's involuntary, it takes over the whole body, and it's very difficult to control. It's called buck fever. Every hunter that I know of who is passionate about what they are doing has it from time to time, some more than others. I've heard other hunters say this and I've said it myself: "If I ever get to the point that I never get excited enough to have buck fever, I'll quit hunting." Buck fever is definitely built out of the passion for the sport of hunting. There are occasions when I just get the feeling that something is about to happen. You must be a hunter to understand this. It's like a sixth sense. That's when buck fever usually happens to me. It starts off slowly and if something actually does happen, it almost gets to the point where it's unsafe to be up in a tree.

It was on an occasion such as this that I missed the opportunity at the only nontypical buck that I've ever actually seen in the wild. It was early on in my bow hunting days and I was on an afternoon hunt on property that I had never hunted before. I had gained permission a few days earlier and placed a ladder stand on the edge of a pasture. I didn't have any time to scout the area and trail cameras had not been invented yet, so I didn't have any idea if there were any nice bucks living in the area. The landowner had told me that he was overrun with deer and that's all I needed to hear. It was during the last hour of daylight. I heard footsteps coming from behind me. I started getting nervous. The sound of the approaching footsteps was getting closer and soon it was right behind me. I began to shake, and buck fever started coming on. I remember thinking that the deer was going to hear my knees knocking together. Then it stepped out in front of me. It was only at about 15 yards. Its rack had so many points that I couldn't begin to count them. It wasn't huge or wide, but it looked like a cluster of tangled vines on its head. I began to shake so violently that it was all I could do to pull my bow back. As I was pulling it back, my arrow started vibrating and making noise. The arrow rests such as we have today had not been invented yet. Just as I was about to be at full draw, my arrow fell off the rest and tumbled to the ground. I realized that I was so shaken that I had been holding the arrow with my finger and when I pulled the bow back the nock came loose from the string. The arrow hit every rung on the ladder stand as it fell to the ground. The "Buck of Many Points" gave me a goodbye blow as he bounded away, never to be seen again. Buck fever cost me the chance at that weird nontypical that day and I remind myself of that experience every time, buck fever starts coming on. Deep breathing and putting things into perspective has helped me to overcome buck fever in the last few years, at least the kind of buck fever that causes me to lose all control. I try to focus more on being thankful for the opportunity to be in God's great creation doing what I love to do. As another hunter reminded me recently, "If it's God's will to send me a monster buck, it will happen." "If it's not His will, it won't." "And He knows what's best."

I was sitting in church recently listening to part two of a two-part sermon about worry and being anxious. It was a wonderful sermon being given by my pastor, Rev. McDonald. All at once, I began to get really nervous, I became extremely flushed and started shaking. I was holding my wife's hand and she could feel me shaking. Here I was having an anxiety attack, right in the middle of the most awesome sermon I had ever heard on the subject. I had never had an anxiety attack, other than buck fever, during my whole life up until about a month prior to this day. This was the third episode. As we were reading the Scripture in Matthew chapter 6, I could hardly see the text in my Bible because I was shaking so badly. I'm not sure what brought this on. Our church was mourning the death of one of our most faithful servants who had just died suddenly a week earlier. We were in the middle of total chaos politically in our nation. We had a pandemic going on that was affecting our church, our church family, and our world. I'm not sure if all of these things combined brought this on or what really. I do know that listening to Rev. McDonald and reading the Scripture helped me to realize that I had been worrying about all of these things more than I had been praying about them and giving them to God. That realization calmed me down and put everything back into perspective. I'm not sure how much of the rest of the sermon that I heard because I was praying without ceasing. I asked God to forgive me for worrying and for trying to fix the world all by myself without His help. I prayed for peace, understanding, and comfort for myself and everyone else. I'm sure that my grip on my wife Johnsie's hand eased up a bit also. The part of the Scripture that hit me the hardest, right in the gut, was in verse 33 where Jesus says, "But seek first the kingdom of God and His righteousness, and all these things shall be added to you". First, not second, not somewhere down the line, but first.

Matthew 6:25–34.

❧ 36 ❧

PLANT AND PRAY

When I was growing up, having a garden wasn't a hobby but rather a necessity. We had a huge garden on the family farm each year. We grew everything from onions and turnips, to tomatoes and potatoes. Going to the grocery store was rare. Between the garden and farm animals, we ate mostly off the land. Each year at garden planting time, the whole family came together to accomplish the task. One thing I can remember that was a constant every time was something that my grandma would say when we finished the planting. She would always say, "well, we've done our part; the rest is up to the Lord." I can only imagine how many prayers my grandma lifted up for rain to water our family garden.

A couple of years ago, I was sweeping some corn kernels off of my back porch. I had stored a couple of bags on the porch to keep it out of the weather until I put it out for the wildlife. Apparently, a squirrel or mouse got on the porch and chewed a hole in the bag.

When I grabbed the bag to take it off of the porch, some of the corn spilled out of the bag. When I swept it off into the flower bed in front of our porch, I had no idea that one of the kernels would take root. I don't know why the others didn't. I accidentally sowed the seed, but I did nothing else to it. God brought the rain, supplied the fertilizer from the decaying mulch, and the sunshine. It grew into a beautiful stalk of corn that ended up having thirteen ears of corn on it. That's only three ears shy of the world record for number of ears on a corn stalk. I've surely never seen that kind of fruit on one corn stalk.

The years that I've been on mission in Alaska, working with kids, have taught me so much about planting seeds for Christ. By being obedient to God's commands to go and do and be the hands and feet of Christ, much fruit has been harvested from seeds that I didn't even know at the time were being planted. Many seeds were planted the first four years that I served with teams in Alaska, but we didn't see any visible fruit. God was watering and fertilizing however and getting those seeds ripe for the harvest. Some of the seeds didn't grow. Whether that is a timing issue on God's part or whether people just denied the truth, I may never know. Some of the seeds were growing for those four years without my knowledge. In the fifth, sixth, and seventh years of our mission in Alaska, some of those seeds had grown into wonderful, beautiful fruit. There were souls saved and baptisms performed. Some of the seeds were growing inside adults that had been touched by how we had shown love to the kids. Some of the seeds had been growing inside the kids for four years. Some of the seeds matured very quickly and became harvestable fruit in just a matter of a few days.

Obeying my wife's command to sweep off our porch resulted in an amazing harvest from a corn stalk when one seed was planted. If we are obedient to Christ's commands and are about the work of sowing seeds of His wonderful truth and love, He will do the rest. Our job is to trust Him and to go forth and sow and pray. Will all the seeds bear fruit? No, they won't. If one does, however, it is worth anything that it might cost us, time, money, talent, heartbreak.

> 2 Corinthians 9:6; Ecclesiastes 11:6; Luke 8:11; Matthew 13:1–58; Galatians 6:7–8.

⁂ 37 ⁂

SOMEONE'S
CALLING MY NAME

My uncle's bird dog Joe, half Irish Setter and half pointer of some sort, was eagerly wagging his tail when I came out of the house with my .410 shotgun. He knew that I was going hunting and he wanted to join me. I surely didn't mind if he tagged along. He was an excellent bird dog and would point rabbits too. I was just a kid and it wasn't unusual at all for me to go out hunting alone. I guess it was somewhat dangerous but somehow it seemed safer for me to go alone. After all, if my gun was accidentally discharged due to tripping over a vine, no one would be around to suffer the consequences. As I've discussed in earlier chapters, it was a different day and time. I could go all over creation hunting and nobody cared. There were no worries about someone kidnapping me. My Daddy always said that if someone ever did kidnap me, they would bring me back soon enough because of how much I ate. Most folks wouldn't be able to afford to feed me. I was woods smart well beyond my age. I had grown up and lived much of my life in the woods and my parents felt comfortable with me being gone for hours while hunting.

Me and ole Joe walked and walked. We came upon a covey of quail at one point and Joe pointed the birds. I eased up through the broom straw and all at once, the quail started getting up. It startled me even though I knew they were going to get up. I shot in their vicinity but didn't hit any of them. Later on, ole Joe pointed a rabbit in his bed, and I connected. We walked this way and that and Joe pointed another rabbit. I got him too. So now I was carrying two rabbits and my shotgun and was getting tired. I sat down for a while and Joe laid down beside me. I began to look around and I realized that I didn't recognize anything that I was seeing. We had been gone for several hours and it was getting late in the day. All our zigzagging through the fields and woods had caused me to be disoriented as to where we were. In other words, we were lost. I'm sure ole Joe wasn't, but he didn't know that I wanted to go home. He just thought it was time to hunt some more. The more I walked, the heavier the rabbits became and the more lost I was. I was beginning to get very concerned. I had never gotten lost before and it was approaching dark. I was about as worried as little boys can be.

It was just a few minutes away from total darkness when I heard what sounded like someone hollering off in the distance. I began to walk that way. As I got closer, I could tell that it was someone calling my name.

I yelled back at the top of my lungs. I ran toward whoever was calling my name. As I got closer, I recognized the voice as that of my Daddy. He was calling my name over and over. Then he started blowing the horn on his truck. Soon, I was at his truck and we loaded Joe in the back and headed home. He was partly angry and partly relieved. He was so upset that he was shaking. He said that he and Mama had been worried sick about me. I was scared that I was going to get a whipping but instead, he and Mama hugged and loved on me when we got home. I ended up being found about a mile from home, but it seemed like a thousand miles when I was lost. Daddy had been riding around the block, stopping to call my name for about an hour. Thank God, I heard him and that he stayed in one place for an extended period of time so that I could get to him.

I've recalled this scary time in my life many times. For years it was just a bad experience that taught me not to wander too far away from home. But after I got saved and began to grow in Christ this experience spoke to me in a much different way. I realized that God had been calling my name for thirty-three years and, like my daddy, He had been waiting for me to answer Him. He had not moved from His location, but I had been wandering all over the place. I had been lost and how sweet it was to be found. Many others are lost in this world right now. Darkness is approaching and, for some, total darkness may be coming soon. He is calling their name. I sure hope and pray that they answer and go to Him.

He is waiting. He will welcome you, like my Mama and Daddy did on that day so long ago, with open arms.

Isaiah 43:1; Luke 15:20.

38

PUSH JESUS UP

———————————————

This chapter will be the most difficult one for me to write because at first glance, it seems as if I'm bringing attention to myself. That isn't the plan and never has been. God gets all the glory. I don't desire or deserve any of the credit. I only answered His call. He did the rest.

I had just arrived home from a mission trip in Alaska. The mission trip was a huge success, but a couple of things were weighing heavily on my mind. I wasn't where I wanted to be physically or spiritually. Due to working seven days a week, twelve hours per day for six months, I had gained weight and was somewhat out of shape. I hadn't had the desire or the energy to do much working out over that time period. Spiritually, I just felt like that I needed for God to give me some-thing major to do, something that would make me have to lean on Him harder than I ever had before. I prayed about both things. I asked God to show me what He wanted me to do to honor Him with my physical body and with my spirit.

God answered my prayers by saying *"get back to basics."* Did I hear his voice? No, I didn't. Did He appear to me in a burning bush? No, He didn't. He just revealed to me, through something that a fellow believer said, how to begin to do what He wanted me to do. I thought to myself, *"what does get back to basics look like?"* Physically, I made a plan to just do basic physical activities. I thought that sit-ups and pushups would be basic and challenging. Spiritually, I just started praying more and reading God's Word. I started doing pushups and sit-ups every day. This went on for less than a week. Then Johnsie and I were heading off to the beach for a week. Our plan was to work out in the gym that was provided at the motel where we were staying.

When we went to the motel gym the first morning of our vacation, I started doing pushups. I had been doing 100 per day. When I completed 100, it was if God said to me "why are you stopping?" It was loud and clear. So, I kept doing pushups. I did 500 that morning. I vowed to Johnsie that I was going to do 500 each day while we were on vacation. She looked at me like I was crazy. I kind of thought I was crazy too. But every day that week, I did 500 pushups. It seemed as if the sit-ups had fallen to the wayside. That was fine with me. I hate doing sit-ups.

The week after we came home from vacation, I continued to do 500 pushups per day. Then in another loud, clear voice, God said to me, "ye of little faith, why are you stopping at 500?" I answered Him by saying, "whaaaaaaaaaaaaaaaaat?" Then it hit me. God was trying to answer my prayer physically and spiritually by getting me to do so many pushups that I couldn't possibly do them without completely relying on Him. "How many, Lord?" "One million in a year," He said. I said again "whaaaaaaaaaaaaaaaaaaaaaaaat?" When I told Johnsie what God had called me to do, she just looked at me with the same expression that I probably had on my face. I was fifty-seven years old and I wasn't at all in the best of shape physically. One million in a year. I quickly started putting a plan together. My thoughts were that I would do my one millionth pushup at Hatcher Pass, Alaska, in July of 2019, exactly one year from when I had left Alaska in 2018. I was making all of these plans when I began to think about the implications of following this call from God. First of all, I had to make sure that it was really a call from Him. It was uncomfortable, impossible for me to do without Him, and I didn't have the tools (body) to accomplish the task. So yes, it was a call from God. Then I started doing some figuring on the calculator. One million in a year. That's 1,000,000 divided by 52 weeks is 19,230.7 divided by 6 days per week is 3,205.1. I had to average 3,205 pushups per day, 6 days a week for 52 weeks. After those calculations, I began to have my doubts about this whole thing. Then I thought, *"well, if I do them seven days a week, I won't have to do as many per day."* God said to me, "do you not have enough faith in me to know that I will be with you?" He revealed to me that He wanted me to take Sundays off, not only to rest but to honor the Sabbath and to show that I had faith in Him. So, 3,205 per day it was. Actually, I had to do a few more each day because the week before, at the beach, I had only done 500 per day.

So, it began. I would get out of bed some mornings at 4:00 A.M. and start doing the pushups. I would do a set, which was only fifteen to twenty-five or so at first, rest for a few seconds (or sometimes minutes) and then do another set. Each time I completed a set, I would punch the number in on my phone's calculator. The first few weeks, it took all day (off and on) to get the required number of pushups in. Then amazingly, rather than get worn out, I got stronger and stronger. After a month or so, I was getting most of the pushups done before noon. All the while, before I started each morning and many times between sets, I would go into my room and close the door to pray. I've been asked why I closed the door since I was mostly alone at home during the day. My answer was this, "Jesus said to do that and I'm taking it literally." So many times, after I had completed a set, I didn't feel like I could do even one more pushup. I would go into my room and pray for strength and come out ready to go at it again. It was like God was healing my weary shoulders, back, and arms in between sets. Soon, I was doing more than what my daily average needed to be. On one particular day, I did more than 10,000 pushups. It was a rainy day and I just kept going all day, stopping only to pray and eat lunch. Each day, I would record in a notebook how many pushups I had completed for that day.

At first no one knew that I was doing this except for Johnsie. Then I began to tell a few of my closest prayer partners. I chose people that I knew would pray for my strength and that understood a calling from God. I felt their prayers and they gave me energy. My ego and pride wanted me to announce to the world what I was doing. God didn't want that. After all, this was a call from Him. He was supplying the energy and determination. He would get the glory. I fought my pride and ego throughout the entire year.

I had to give up much of my normal lifestyle in order to continue to press forward with this calling. I didn't hunt much during that deer season, especially in the mornings. I would walk down to my pond occasionally and fish for a few minutes, but I felt as if God kept telling me that His calling was priority and that if I wanted Him to get me through it, I had to give up some things. I gave up the fitness class that I had been going to with Johnsie for several years. I missed it. I gave up my daily midday naps in my recliner. All my thoughts and efforts had to be focused on this calling, this mission. Some days were really difficult. After several months of this, I began to get a little discouraged. I began to think that I was going through all of this and nobody really cared. That was satan trying to stop me. He was trying to get me to turn my attention to self. I started telling a few more people what I was doing. I honestly think I did that so that maybe I would get a few pats on the back. Mostly, I just got the kind of looks from people that make you feel as if you are crazy or that they don't believe you. I'm not going to lie: it was very challenging emotionally and mentally. Some days were worse than others. I cried all the different kinds of tears at times. I felt sorry for myself because no one was acknowledging my accomplishments at times. I felt so humble by God's awesome mercy and grace that it brought me to tears at times. My shoulders hurt so bad at times that I would tear up a bit. Prayer got me through all these times.

When I reached the 500,000 and 750,000 goals, it started to feel like that this could really happen. I might be able to complete this task with God's help. I remember calculating my daily average and was very surprised to see that I was way ahead of schedule. I was on schedule to complete the 1,000,000 pushups sometime in June. That was an entire month early. I started trying to do somewhere around the initial daily average of 3,205 per day. I didn't want to take days off. I was too close to actually accomplishing this to back off.

I began to share my goal with the Alaska mission team. I had a burning desire to share what I had been doing with the world. I started posting on social media the hashtag #pushJesusup. It was a subtle attempt to put it out there without coming out and announcing what God had called me to do. I think, subconsciously, it was an attempt to get attention. But God said no. I was confused. I didn't understand how I could give God the glory in all of this if people didn't know anything about it. I wanted to shout to the world what He was allowing me to do. I shared this with my prayer partner/friend Stacey, and she told me this. "God will give you the opportunity to share and honor Him in all of this in His time. He will let you know how and when." Perhaps, right now, in this book, is the how and when. I don't know what I was expecting. I guess, I thought that all the media outlets would be knocking on my door wanting to do a story on my incredible feat. All of that was the battle with self, showing its ugly head again. God never said that he was going to make me a hero or that I would become a household name throughout the land or anything of the sort. He told me that He would give me what I needed to accomplish His call and that He would be by my side the whole way. How God gets glorified in it is up to Him.

On June 20, 2019, I completed my pushup 999,998. That was over a month early. I couldn't fathom that God had allowed me to do this. My new goal was to do 1 more pushup on my birthday, July 21, and then do the last pushup on top of the world at the summit in Hatcher Pass, Alaska, on the eve of July 30. I didn't do any more pushups until my birthday, when I slowly completed pushup 999,999. Johnsie recorded me doing it in slow motion.

On July 30, 2019, in Hatcher Pass, Alaska, I, along with several of my friends and fellow missionaries, began the climb to the top of the summit in the pouring rain. With no other opportunity to come back another day, we made the grueling climb to the top. Soaking wet and cold, we made it to the top. Before I did my 1,000,000th pushup, I facetimed my wife Johnsie back home so that she could see me bring this year-long call to completion. She had to be there in some way because she had been my cheerleader, my shoulder, my encouragement, and my drill sergeant throughout the whole year. My friend Meghan surprised me with a sleeveless tee shirt that she had made for me that said Quest for 1,000,000, #pushJesusup. I put it on right there in front of God and everybody. Did I mention that it was cold up there? About that time, the skies opened up, the fog and rain disappeared, and the most awesome rainbow that I have ever seen lit up the sky. God was showing me that He had fulfilled His promise to me. I did the pushup. We all prayed together, a prayer of thanksgiving, I told Johnsie that I loved her and hung up the phone. We all started back down the mountain and the rain began to pour again. We were all drenched and cold when we got back to the van, but we didn't care. God had shown us who He is.

So, what was the purpose of the call? I'm not totally sure. Maybe so that I could give God the glory in this book. I know that I stayed on my knees for a full year and had a deep personal relationship with Him for that entire time. Maybe that was the purpose. Or perhaps, He just wanted to test my faith. He will reveal His purpose to me when He wants to. I may never know until I get home. That's alright with me. If I could share one word that would represent this year long call, it would be humility. I surely was humbled by my limited abilities without Him and the unlimited possibilities with Him. I hope that the lyrics below will set the stage for the kind of humility that we all must have in order to serve Him. God gave me these words and music to a song a few years ago that was the most difficult song I've ever written. Why? Because in this song, I had to admit what I truly am without Him.

What I Am

So unworthy, so unclean
A beast before Thee
The least of these,

Father, I know just what I am.
Father, I know; Father, I know.

Tried to cleanse my own heart
Wash my hands without You;
A filthy rag
Was the best I could do.

Father, I know just what I am
Father, I know; Father, I know.

My flesh is a failure
No matter what I do.
You are the strength of my heart, Lord,
I'm drawing nearer to You.

Father, I know just what I am.
Father, I know; Father I know.

I'm nothing on my own, Lord,
Now I know it's true.
My hope, my faith, my trust, Lord,
Is all in You.
Father, I know just what I am.
Father, I know; Father I know.

Father, I know what I am
Father, change me,
Make me, and mold me
To be what You would have me to be.
Amen

Exodus 33:14; John 14:16; Philippians 4:19; 2
Corinthians 5:7; Isaiah 40:29, 31: 41:10; 43:2.

39

ADDICTION CONTROL

A ddictions—everybody has at least one. From the time I was old enough to walk, the outdoors became my addiction. Hunting, fishing, searching for artifacts, and anything else that you could do outdoors as a little boy in North Carolina were all my passions. I worked outside on the tobacco farm. When the work was done, I played outside. All of my hobbies had to do with outdoor activity. As I got older, the passions became addictions. Hunting and fishing became my priorities. When I got home from school, I grabbed a gun, a cane pole, or fishing rod. My beagles knew when I got off the bus that we were about to go hunting every afternoon during hunting season. My schoolwork often suffered as a result. I didn't care about being social. Honestly, back in those days there wasn't much social activity anyway. I only had my cousins and the Rogers boys down the road to play with. We would sometimes play a game of basketball or football. Mostly though, it was just me by myself in the woods or by Granddaddy's pond. It seemed as if everything I did revolved around my outdoor activities.

As I got older, I played football and baseball on the school teams. They took up much of my time but whenever I wasn't at practice or at a game it was back to the woods and water. Then, of course, I became interested in girls. Somehow, I managed to date a little and hunt and fish a lot. Looking back, that was probably a good thing. The point here is that I was still addicted to the outdoors and it was still my priority.

When Johnsie and I started dating, I quickly fell in love. From day one, she knew that I loved the outdoors and from then until now she has always supported me in my love for the outdoors. She has never had any desire to hunt. She likes to fish on occasion for a few minutes if she is catching something. She has never tried to get me to stop doing what I love to do, however. After we got married, I remember telling her one day that she knew that she was marrying a hunter and fisherman and that I would be spending a lot of time doing it. She said, "yep, I know." I have never had any of the addictions that so many people have with alcohol, drugs, or other things. but I had addictions, nevertheless. When my children Anna and Shane came along, I spent way too much time feeding my passion and not enough time at home helping to raise them. That's something I surely regret. The night that Shane was born, I was frog gigging at the pond across from my parents' house. I can still hear my daddy hollering at me from his back porch,

"Johnsie is about to have that baby." Lord, he was right too. I barely got her to the hospital in time.

When I got saved at the age of thirty-three a lot of things changed. I still loved hunting and fishing, but I wasn't completely obsessed or addicted anymore. As Shane got older, I started taking him on all of my outdoor rendezvous. Anna, like Johnsie, just never got bit by the hunting and fishing bug. There have been times when food has been my addiction. You can look at my belly and see that. There have been times when Johnsie was my addiction. My outdoor hobbies still have a tendency to be an addiction. It seems as if whatever the addiction, I always somehow find time and money to feed them. The truth of the matter is that when I've made Jesus my addiction and my priority, all these things have been available in abundance. God knows my heart's desires and He desires that my heart would first love Him.

Wouldn't it be amazing if everyone's addiction was Jesus? Can you imagine everyone somehow finding a way to be fed spiritually on Sunday? Everyone would bypass the biscuit places and rush to church. Boats would be parked and guns would be hanging in the safe, because everyone would set aside that day for worship of The King. The stores would be closed because nobody would shop on the Lord's day. My granddaddy used to say that "the good Lord gave us six days to hunt and fish and all these other things that we're interested in, so today (Sunday) we need to rest and worship Him."

That's good advice that I try but struggle to live by. God can and will provide strength to walk away from any worldly addiction if we let Him.

Proverbs 25:28; Titus 2:11–12; 1 Corinthians 10:13; 1 John 2:16; Matthew 6:33.

⚜ 40 ⚜

LET US PRAY

Anyone who has ever hunted with me knows that the last thing we do before we head to the woods is pray. I feel that it is vital and necessary. On most occasions, I do the praying but on one particular afternoon as we were about to head in opposite directions to our deer stands, I asked my grandson Levi to pray. This is what he prayed. "Lord, thank You for the opportunity to hunt and to enjoy Your creation. Thank You for all Your blessings. Lord, if it is in Your will, please send us a big buck and let our aim be good. But Lord, even if You don't, we will still thank You and love You anyway." *We thank You and love You anyway.* That's quite an awesome prayer for a young man to pray.

Levi said this prayer during a confusing time in our nation. It was an election year and the outcome of the election, national and state, was much different than what I had prayed for. It was causing turmoil all over the world. Many Christians had prayed for candidates who were Prolife and stood for God designed marriages and so on and so on. It seemed as if liberal minded candidates won in most cases. I was surely upset about what laws might be changed or legislated in. I was concerned about the future of our state and nation. What upset me more than anything however is the way that many Christians were behaving. Instead of faithfully understanding that God had allowed all of these people to be elected for some purpose, some seemed to lose their faith. Instead of like Levi prayed, "Lord we thank You and love You anyway," many were saying "God, what are you doing?" It would be a good thing for these Christians to read the book of Habakkuk in the Old Testament. He was asking God what He was doing and actually complaining to God about why He was allowing things to go on. God pretty much told him that He wasn't going to tell him. That's good enough for me. I surely don't know God's reasons for allowing these things, but I surely trust that He is in control.

Getting back to prayer. On one occasion, I was asked to pray for an individual who had just been diagnosed with cancer. I added this young lady to my list and prayed for her immediately. My prayer list was long and getting longer every day. My cup was running over with prayer opportunities. When someone asks me to pray for them, I consider it a great honor and privilege that they would have enough confidence in me to even ask. I get quite disturbed however at something that I see on social media almost every day. Someone will put out a prayer request and immediately, one after another, folks start replying with prayers, praying, or I will pray. There's nothing wrong with that, but here's a word of caution so that maybe you won't fall into the same trap that I did. I found myself posting things such as "I will pray for you" or "lifting you up" and the like. The problem is that many times, I didn't actually pray for these folks or situations. It was only lip service. I believe that prayer is the most powerful tool that God has given us and that there is no privilege greater than being able to go to God on someone else's behalf. But saying that you will pray and not actually doing it has no power at all. That's why we don't see more miracles from God. God doesn't honor lip service.

Also, those of us who are saved by His grace need to repent every single time before we petition Him about anything. God said that He would hear and answer the prayers of the righteous. The only thing that makes any of us righteous is the forgiveness that God provides. When I pray, I surely want Him to hear me and answer me in His time. I made a promise to God that before I respond to anyone with "praying for you," "prayers," "lifting you up" or anything of the sort; I would actually pray. My responses now on social media are always things such as "just lifted you up" or "just prayed about this and will continue." Whenever anyone asks me to pray, I will pray with all my heart that they will be healed, that their troubles will be lifted off of them, and that God will intervene in their situation and show them His grace, His mercy, and His love. And I know, because He said so, that if we ask, we shall receive. I also know that He expects us to be about His work as we are praying and that every prayer we pray should begin with "Lord, if it's in Your will,..."

The Bible has so much to say about prayer including "pray without ceasing." Below are a few things that God has revealed to me about prayer:

- You can't bring me down while I'm lifting you up.
- Expectation must be preceded by prayer or it isn't valid.
- I believe that God must be saying something like this: "you continue to petition me, but how can I help or assist you when you aren't doing and won't do, anything?"
- If you truly want to stand tall, you must spend a considerable amount of time on your knees.

I believe that God answers prayers in three ways: yes, no, or wait. I also believe that, as we mature in Christ and become more like Him, we will be more in His will when we pray. When we are more in His will in our prayers, we will automatically get yes answers more often. What a great knowledge of His greatness.

I'm so thankful that all my grandchildren know how to pray and aren't ashamed to pray in front of anyone. My two youngest granddaughters, Ellie and Alyvia, say the simplest prayers that are so powerful and special. They don't have any of the world's worries or prejudices or any of that stuff to get in the way of praying exactly what's on their hearts. My older grand-daughters, Emmie and Alayna, say touching, heartfelt prayers that make me tear up. And Levi, well he has been saying amazing prayers since he was a very small boy. I remember him, at eight years old, praying every night for weeks before he went on his first mission trip to Alaska. My son Shane and his wife Amanda and my daughter Anna and her husband Drew, have instilled in my grandchildren that prayer is important. I am so very thankful for that.

Do you love Him anyway? Even if He says no or "I'm not going to tell you," do you still trust Him? Do you still have faith that He knows best? God said, "not today" to Levi's prayer for Him to send us a big buck on that November afternoon, but because Levi loved Him anyway, a few days later, He answered Levi's prayer with a big yes and sent him a truly big buck. Levi's aim was true, and his heart was also.

1 Thessalonians 5:16–18; 1 John 5:14–15; 2 Chronicles 7:14; Ephesians 6:18; Jeremiah 29:12; James 5:13; Mark 11; 24; Matthew 5:44; Proverbs 15:8.

41

BE STILL

I've probably said it like a million times, "be still." I said it so much when Shane and I were hunting when he was a little boy. If a deer came out, I would whisper over and over, "be still, be still, be still." Even if he wasn't moving, I'd still say it. It was the same with Levi when he was first starting hunting with me. Now my granddaughters have to hear me say it. With a couple of my granddaughters, it's a requirement every ten seconds the whole time we are hunting.

It was one of those days when I had so much to do that I didn't know where to begin. I had so many irons in the fire and I was, quite frankly, frustrated. When I get frustrated, there's not much need for me to try and accomplish any task because I will surely mess things up or do something wrong. I decided that I wasn't going to get anything accomplished until my mood changed. When I get like that, going to the woods or to the water is the only solution. There, I can focus and talk to God and hopefully get back on track. I have a special place down by the creek where I like to go and pray, read my Bible, and build a small fire to sit by. So off I went. I took my Bible, some fire-starting items (toilet paper rolls, lint from the dryer, and matches), and a couple of bottles of water in my backpack.

I arrived at my special place and started a small fire. I said a prayer and then opened my Bible. I didn't have any particular Scripture in mind, so I just let God decide what He wanted me to read. My Bible opened up to the book of Psalms. I began to read and soon I was at chapter 37 verse 7 that reads, "Be still before the Lord and wait patiently for Him; fret not yourself over the one who prospers in his way; over the man who carries out evil devices." I kept reading and came upon chapter 46 verse 10 that reads, He says "Be still and know that I am God; I will be exalted in the earth." Wow, God was surely trying to tell me something here. I had been so busy with life and all the things that really aren't important, that I had forgotten to be still and let God deal with my heart. I will never forget the release of tension at that moment. I don't think that I have ever felt so relaxed and peaceful. God wanted me to slow down, be still for a moment and listen to Him. He also wanted me to let Him handle all the things that were causing me to be frustrated and agitated.

This might seem strange, but I felt a connection to my Cherokee ancestors while I was sitting by the fire. I wasn't trying to get in touch with spirits but rather The Spirit and I had surely made contact with Him. I heard

God saying over and over in my mind "be still, be still, be still" and I began to pray. This is the prayer that I lifted up to Him right there at the fire by the creek.

> Father, you keep telling me over and over, "be still and know that I am God." So today, my prayer is not that You bring something new, amazing, or miraculous into my life. My prayer today, Lord, is that you would use me where I am. You have allowed me to be where I am or You have caused me to be where I am. Either way, Lord, help me to be content with that, to rejoice in that. I only desire to please You, Jesus. Help me to get myself out of the way, so that I may be in Your will. Transform the desires of my flesh into an eternal desire to be of and about You. Father, I pray this prayer for all of my brothers and sisters as well, Amen.

I am reminded of this day quite frequently. Admittedly, I let life get to me way too often. I am not still often enough. I know that. Some days, I just need to grab my Bible and my backpack and head to the fire by the creek.

Psalm 37:7; 46:10; 131:2; Exodus 14:14.

❈ 42 ❈

A TANGLED WEB

I t was early bow season, and I was going to try a morning hunt. I had a really nice buck on camera that had been showing up about an hour after daylight. I grabbed my bow and a small flashlight and headed off toward my stand. It seemed that every few feet along the path leading to my deer stand, I ran into a spider web. The spiders like to build their webs from one side of the path to the other. My small flashlight just didn't provide enough illumination to keep me from constantly getting tangled in the webs. By the time I reached my deer stand, I was covered in webs. Then a huge garden spider, which seemed as big as a frisbee, crawled across my face. I'm not one who has arachnophobia but I'm not very fond of them crawling on me either. If it had been my daughter Anna, she would have screamed, and the hunt would have been over.

Whenever I take one of my grandchildren or another kid hunting, I always shine the light in front of them so that they can see where they are going. God says that we should let our light shine before men so that they will see our good deeds and glorify our Father in heaven. There's a challenge in this for me. Am I letting my light shine for Jesus so that these kids can see that I am about good deeds in the name of my Savior?

This got me to thinking about how this world only offers complete darkness or at best ineffective, artificial light (like my little flashlight), for us to walk by. Without the light of Jesus Christ, we will become entangled in the many webs of this life. But there is light to replace the darkness, a light for our path, a lamp for our feet. Jesus is the light that shines in the darkness and darkness cannot overcome it. Jesus said that He was the light of the world and that whoever follows Him will never walk in darkness but will have the light of life. What great promises.

I have never liked being in the dark. Evil resides in darkness. It seems as if most criminals operate in darkness. I'm not a fan of walking to my deer stand or to a turkey blind in the dark. I thank God for giving me the one and only true light, Jesus Christ, to light the path so that I may know which direction to walk in and so that I can fully see the webs of this life and can resist being entangled.

Matthew 4:16; 5:16; John 1:5; 8:12; 9:5; 18:28; 119:105.

43

HE AIN'T DONE WITH ME YET

Have you ever felt inadequate as a hunter? I surely have. I've had days when I just didn't think I had any idea what I was doing. Just like all hunters, I've come home empty handed much more than I've been successful. I spent an entire turkey season trying to harvest one mature gobbler. Every single time I went after him, no matter whether it was a morning, midday, or afternoon hunt, he would gobble and gobble but never come in. I tried setting up where he roosted the evening before and he would fly up just out of range. I probably had fifty encounters with him. It seemed as if he was just playing a game with me. On the last day of the season, I eased into the woods near a creek in the vicinity of where he had been roosting night after night. I didn't make a single call and I didn't put out a decoy. Just before last light, I heard something walking in the leaves, headed toward me. Soon I saw that colorful head bobbing through a thicket. He walked right in front of me at 20 yards and I smoked him. After an entire season of defeat and feeling as if I didn't know anything at all about turkey hunting, I now felt like the greatest turkey hunter in the world. I had outsmarted him.

In June of 2016, I found out that after thirty-seven years, my position at work was being cut. I don't care who you are, how strong you are, or how prepared you are, this kind of news will rock your world. Even though I knew better, I began to feel used up, devalued, and my sense of worth was shattered. Thank God, in time, all of that got better.

What I didn't realize was that these feelings of inadequacy, and unworthiness had spilled over into my spiritual life. For about a year, I had fallen into the trap of feeling like I was all used up for God, that He couldn't use me anymore. I know now that it was all foolishness, but it was happening, and these were real feelings. I was going through all of the motions but was somewhat spiritually flatlined.

In August of 2017, I half-heartedly arrived in Alaska for our annual mission trip. We arrived on Sunday and began our park ministry on Monday. I did what I was asked to do but my heart just didn't seem to be in it. I felt like just another body to make it look like we had a big team. Then on Thursday, in the park, God slapped me right in the face and said, "who are you to tell me that I can't use you anymore?" On that day, God used me, this filthy, doubting rag, to lead a young lady to Christ.

I was in so much awe of Him. I was overwhelmed with joy and blessing.

Realizing what had happened, Friday morning I went to the altar at the church where we were staying before anyone else was awake. I thanked God for what had transpired, and I told Him that I was willing to be used again. I asked Him to use me however He wanted to. Friday afternoon, in the park, God allowed me to lead three more young people to Christ. These weren't kids that I had made a strong connection with during the week; they weren't the ones that I thought God might use me on. He, in ways that only He could have set up, sent each one of these kids to me and placed them on their knees. He knew that they were ripe for the harvest. He gave me exactly the right words to say to them in leading them in the sinner's prayer.

There were many people who had a role in these young people coming to know Christ. An answered calling by my brother in Christ, Jay Dagenhart, years before was the only reason that any of us from my church started coming on mission in Alaska. I thank God so much for that. I also believe that God knew all about this when He stationed my Daddy in Alaska when he served in the Army. My promise to Daddy was the initial reason that I came on my first mission trip to Alaska. The other members of my team, the teams that came before us and the leaders and staff of the GraceWorks, Alaska ministry all played a part. Yet, God sent me to be the instrument that He used to lead these three children to salvation in Christ. I'll never be able to fully grasp what transpired that week. Why did He use me? Perhaps, He just wanted me to know that He valued me and that He could, would, and was ready to use me.

I was, and still am, restored and willing. My God is ready to use me and my God is ready to use you. Instead of *"why me, Lord,"* it is now *"why not me, Lord?"* God didn't take my job away; He didn't take my worth away; and no man or company did either. He set me up to be ready to be used. All He required of me was to be willing.

> **Philippians 2:12–13; Jeremiah 29:11; Ephesians 2:10; Romans 8:28; Hebrews 13:21; Isaiah 43:4; Luke 12:6–7.**

⇥ 44 ⇤

As Kids Go

<hr>

Watching my grandchildren play in the creek, looking for fool's gold and salamanders, reminded me of when I was a little boy. There was one particular time when my cousin was supposed to come and spend the night with me. The plan was for us to go down to the freshwater spring in the pasture and catch crayfish, crawdads, or as we called them, crawfish. There were always a few crawfish down in the cement pipe that had been placed over the spring by my granddaddy many years before. The spring used to be the water supply for the family when my daddy was growing up. I've heard him talk about hauling buckets of water from the spring on many occasions. Now it was the drinking supply for our cows when they were on that end of the pasture. There was a pond on the other end. The night my cousin came, we hardly slept at all because we were so excited about catching those crawfish. I have no idea what our plans were for them. I didn't know back in that day that they were delicious when cooked. I think just the adventure of trying to catch them without getting pinched was the attraction. The next morning when we woke up and looked outside, it was pouring rain and my daddy said that it was supposed to rain like that all day. I was completely crushed. Adults sometimes have a hard time understanding why little things mean so much to kids, and my parents didn't understand why I was so upset. They made all kinds of cool suggestions of things that we could do but nothing could fix my broken heart that day. It was as if it were the end of the world.

My thoughts came back to my grandkids playing in the creek. We were on our annual adventure of walking through the woods on our property, exploring the creek, and looking for treasures. Treasures include anything from turtle shells to bird feathers and shed deer antlers to pretty rocks. We usually build a campfire and have lunch in the woods. There is a very steep hill that the kids will slide down, struggle to climb back up, and then slide down again. This has become the main attraction. I overheard one of the girls say at one point that this was "better than Disney World." I don't know about that but they sure were having fun. As strange as it may seem, other than Christmas, this has become the most anticipated day of the year for our family.

Simple things are what kids will remember about their childhood. I'm concerned about the kids of today and what they spend most of their time doing. So much of their time is spent in front of a tablet, computer, or phone screen. Even books, I believe, take up too much of kids' lives in some cases. What kids need more of is outdoors: being in the sunshine, getting dirty, and learning about God's creation and life. Kids of today get upset when their electronic toys get broken or the internet isn't working properly. When I was a kid, I got upset when my tobacco stick ran out of gas. I rode that stick for many, many miles. Every now and then, when I would get tired, I would pull up to the back steps to pretend like I was filling up with gas. Most of the time it was at Grandma's back steps and while my tobacco stick was getting filled up, I would go in and Grandma would refuel me with my favorite: peach Jell-O. Kids don't seem to be allowed to be kids anymore. Kids need to be allowed to make mistakes so that they will learn. They need to be disciplined in some other way than taking an electronic device away or having to stand in a corner. I won't argue about that. It's biblical. Most of all, they need to see parents and grandparents serving God, reading God's Word, and praying. We live in a society today that has made almost everything and anything more important than Jesus. Kids are smarter than we might think. They watch and see what things we prioritize in our lives. Below is a very narrow list of things that seem to have become more important than teaching our kids about Jesus in the ordinary household of today.

I'm afraid that we've made material things so important that our kids will miss Jesus!

I'm afraid that we've made politics so important that our kids will miss Jesus!

I'm afraid that we've made our rights, and being right, so important that our kids will miss Jesus!

I'm afraid that we've made money so important that our kids will miss Jesus!

I'm afraid that we've made education so important that our kids will miss Jesus!

I'm afraid that we've made sports so important that our kids will miss Jesus!

PARENTS: make Jesus so important that our kids won't miss anything!

I'm so very thankful that my children, Anna and Shane, and their spouses Drew and Amanda, make sure that Jesus is the most important thing in their household. I thank God for that every day. The fruit of that can be seen in mine and Johnsie's grandchildren. Levi, Emmie, and Alayna, the three oldest, have accepted Christ as their Savior and have been baptized and the two little ones, Ellie and Alyvia, talk about Jesus all the time. The four girls sing at church almost every Sunday and Levi helps run the sound system. They all are involved in other activities and do very well in them, but God comes first. What are you making a priority in your household? If it isn't Jesus, it's not too late. Today is a great day and in the famous words of my daddy, "too late is a terrible thing."

Proverbs 17:6; 22:6; 29:17; Isaiah 54:13; Psalm 127:3; Matthew 18:1–3; 19:14; 3 John 1:4; Ephesians 6:4; Mark 10:15–16.

⊰ 45 ⊱

FIRSTS

It was the first time that I had ever been fishing. I don't remember much about it except that I was only about three or four years old. My granddaddy Denny took me behind the dam of what is supposedly the oldest natural lake in North Carolina: Chub Lake. I'm not sure how anyone could truly know that but that's what has always been told. Granddaddy baited my hook with a red wiggler and helped me throw my line out. I can still see that cork going under, and he told me to "pull it up." I yanked upward on that cane pole and caught my first fish ever. It was a small bream, but it was the world record to me and Granddaddy. I can still see his big smile. The fishing excursion was over. We had to go back to Grandma and Granddaddy's house right then and show Grandma my fish. That is a memory that is etched in my mind forever and the moment that got me "hooked" on fishing. I've had the privilege of being with all my grandchildren when they caught their first fish.

There are so many firsts in my love for the outdoors that have been special to me. My first deer, my first buck, first turkey, and so on. All of those firsts, essentially, are why I am so passionate about hunting. I've been sitting beside several young folks as they harvested their first bucks. Shane's first squirrel, first buck, and first turkey have permanent markers in my mind and on my heart. I have the video and pictures of Levi's first buck. I hope and pray that I will get to have a part in all my granddaughters' firsts.

One of the firsts in my life eventually led to the second greatest decision I've ever made. Of course, the greatest decision was accepting Christ as my savior. The second greatest was asking Johnsie to share my life with me forever. It was a beautiful Sunday morning. We were having old fashioned day at church. Everyone was to dress like the days of old and such. My cousin Amy and I rode her old mule, Ruth, to church. It was about a mile ride, and I was ready to get off ole Ruth when we got there. However, when we arrived in the parking lot, I spotted the prettiest girl I had ever seen. I was in a daze and just stayed on ole Ruth, staring at this beautiful young girl with pigtails. Here I was sitting on a mule, looking ridiculous, completely and helplessly in love. Yes, I do believe in love at first sight. It sure happened with me. I had never seen this girl before. We finally got off the mule and tied her up. I found out that this vision of loveliness had been invited by a girl that went to our church. I learned that she was twelve years old and that her name was Johnsie. The song, "The First Time Ever I Saw Your Face," reminds me of this moment every time I hear it. I went up to this ray of sunshine and began to talk to her. I was almost fifteen years old and she just turned twelve. I didn't care, but her parents did. They wouldn't let me call her or anything. I was crushed and didn't understand at the time, but I certainly do now. I never forgot her or that first glance at that pretty little girl with pigtails. Almost four years later, she was a guest at our church again. I went and sat with her during the service and we've been together ever since. That was forty-one years ago.

Two firsts that I am in total awe of every time I think about them happened in Alaska while I was on mission. I lead my first person to Christ, in Palmer, Alaska, while on mission for Christ in a neighborhood park. This young lady was eleven years old at the time and came up to me after a Bible study time that we had just had with all of the kids at the park. She said that she wanted to give her life to Jesus. We knelt down in the grass and I explained everything to her and made sure that she knew what she was doing. Then I led her in the sinner's prayer. I'm so thankful that God chose me to be the instrument of His love and allowed me to lead this special young lady to Him. Her name is Ariana and the following year she brought her sister to me, and I lead her to Christ. The year after that, she brought her friend to me, and I led him to Christ. I have stayed in touch with this wonderful young lady and I know that because of this first that God gave me, she is going to do great things for Him. I also performed my first baptism in that same park the following year. I had led three young people to Christ the summer that Ariana got saved and I was burdened that they had not been baptized. I started asking questions about whether we could somehow baptize these kids during our upcoming summer mission trip in the same park. I was told that we could, but I needed to get permission from parents. I started working on that and got permissions. When we arrived in Alaska, I was told that a pastor was going to perform the baptisms. God worked things out the way He wanted, however, and gave that pastor another job for that night. I was allowed to perform the baptisms as I have explained in another chapter. The first one I baptized that night was a young man named Jaden. He was a special young man that God allowed me to lead to Christ a year earlier. That first baptism is something that I surely will never forget. Jaden went under water, in a horse trough, and came out a new creature. Hallelujah is what one of the GraceWorks staff shouted when he came up out of that water. And all God's people said, Amen.

One thing that we always tell the people of Alaska when we are on mission is that we love them because God first loved us. That is the greatest first that ever has or ever will be. God sent his firstborn son, Jesus to die for us on the cross. God gave, and still gives us, the first fruits—the best of the crop—His son Jesus.

In turn, we should bring Him our firsts, our best. We should tithe first, before our money does anything else. We should give Him our talents and gifts first, before anyone else benefits from them. You see, God put us first and we, not only should, but are commanded to put Him first. Hunting and fishing firsts make great memories. Spiritual firsts, now those are something you can hang your hat on.

Romans 8:23, 29; I Corinthians 15:20; I John 4:19.

46

My Testimony

W hy have I gone this deep into the book without giving my testimony? I'm not totally sure. Maybe, it's hurtful. Maybe, I'm a little ashamed. Maybe, it's difficult to put myself out there for the whole world to see. I actually decided that now is the right time this past Sunday in church. I don't know what sparked the fire but once the fire started, our pastor threw plenty of fuel on it during his sermon. I began to think about my testimony and what God would have me share. My whole life is a testimony, and every chapter of this book is a part of it. I am going to attempt to share what I think will be useful to others and what will glorify God.

When I was a little boy, my parents didn't go to church. They were good people, and both had been saved years earlier. For whatever reasons, life had taken them away from church. Mama talked about Jesus a lot but that was about the extent of it. My grandma took me to church when I was a toddler. Granddaddy would drive us there and then come back to pick us up. I grew up like that for several years. Church on Sunday with Grandma; Sunday school and worship service. When I became a teenager, I joined the youth group at church. I had the choice of going to youth activities at church or working. My daddy had recently given up drinking alcohol on the weekends and had truly become a different person. He and Mama started attending church and they helped as leaders of the youth. In those days, we didn't have paid or appointed youth leaders. The parents of the youth filled that role. I think that was a good thing. I feel like that during this time is when my daddy really got saved. We attended church and were involved with youth activities and a few building and grounds activities. This went on for about a year or so.

Then, at a revival service one night when I was fifteen years old, I walked the aisle and joined the church. I had a fuzzy feeling inside and went on to get baptized a couple of weeks later. I was one of those boys who Mamas like to brag about. I was one of those "don't do" boys. I didn't do a lot of things that some of the other teenagers were doing. I didn't experiment with things that were not considered godly. I didn't do this, and I didn't do that, so it looked like I was truly a saved child of God. I spent my time doing things that were productive. I was a hard worker. All of the things that a parent could want in a child, I seemed to be about. It was almost as if I had joined a cult called "don't do these things." I was considered to be odd by most of the other teenagers that I knew because I was pretty much a loner and wasn't about most of the things that they were about. I played sports, worked out a lot, hunted, and fished. All pretty good things for a teenage boy to be about. Did you notice that I never mentioned praying or reading the Bible? Did you notice that I never once said that I witnessed to any of these other teenagers or anybody else? On the outside, I appeared to be the model Christian young man but other than a long list of *don't do*'s, there was no evidence to be found that I had become a new creature.

There were many non-Christian behaviors that were exhibited in my life over the next few years. Johnsie and I got married. She knew me. She knew everything about me, but she loved me in spite of that and saw something in me. We went to church almost every Sunday. Anna and Shane came along, and I was a good daddy and husband. Notice I said good and not godly. There is a huge difference between a good daddy and husband and a godly one. I was providing for them. I loved them, but I wasn't supplying their greatest need: for me to be the spiritual leader in the home. Soon, using a preacher that I didn't like as an excuse, I stopped going to church. On Sunday mornings I went fishing or claimed that I had too much to do because I worked so much at the power plant. This went on for a long while. I honestly don't know how long. Thank God, Johnsie kept going to church and took the kids with her every Sunday. I'm so grateful that she didn't nag me about it or judge me. She simply asked every Sunday morning, "do you want to go to church with us this morning." She was so nonjudgmental and humble. She would always come home and tell me that so and so asked about me and would tell me about the sermon and the readings. One Sunday morning, I overheard Shane ask her, "why do I have to go to church, Daddy doesn't go?" This hit me hard. It moved me but it didn't move me enough. I still didn't go. Then, a few days later, Johnsie told me that she really missed me going to church with her because it seemed as if that was the only place where we were able to go together. I worked so much that it was rare for us to be able to go anywhere together. We barely made ends meet, so we didn't go out to eat and things such as that. I began to think really hard about what she had said and what Shane had said. I began to search myself and look into the mirror at what I had become. I loved my kids and Johnsie more than anything but I felt like I wasn't doing my part.

The words that my kids and wife had said along with many other things: a lifetime of prayers lifted up by my grandparents, parents, and Johnsie, people who kept nagging me about my spiritual life, preachers, teachers, and a host of life-altering events, put me on my knees in the most unusual place. At 3:30 A.M. on an April morning, standing naked as a jaybird, covered in coal dust, in the locker room of the power plant where I worked, I asked Jesus (for real) to come into my life and save me. I wept tears of humility, shame, and then joy. I asked God to please forgive me. I told Him that I could not handle life on my own and that I needed Him to take control. I asked Him to show me what I needed to do to be a godly (not good) husband and father. I went in the shower and got truly baptized. As that nasty coal dust left my body, so did the sin. It all went down the drain, never to be seen again. As the soap and bath cloth cleansed my body, Jesus cleansed my soul. That experience at fifteen was just what I had described it to be, a fuzzy feeling. That baptism back then was nothing more than a time of getting wet. It didn't happen for me at church. It didn't happen to me at a Bible study. It happened in my nakedness, as filthy as a person can possibly be, at an odd hour in a place that was noisy and nasty.

My walk with the Lord has been a rocky one just like everyone else's. I struggle every day to be the servant that He would have me be and to be about the plan He has for my life. I fail and I stumble, but He always holds out His hand for me to grab hold of and gets me back on my feet. I am thankful for my church and for godly friends. I'm thankful for a godly family who never gave up on me.

Shane came to me several years ago with a tune that he had come up with on his guitar. He wanted me to put some lyrics to the music. That's a tough challenge for a songwriter. Most of my songs were created when I had my guitar in my hands and God gave me the words and music simultaneously. I began to think that I had never really given my testimony in one of my songs, so

I sat down and started to write. Below are the lyrics to the song that became one of the favorites whenever we performed with our band, Stumble No More.

Something About This Man

When I was a child in Sunday school,
My teacher told me all about the golden rule.
She showed me in the Bible, it was written in red
Just one of the many things that Jesus said.;
Then I remember, later down the road
I was carrying a heavy load
Jesus stepped in and took me by the hand
That's when I started thinking, "there's something about this man."
I didn't want to swallow my pride
And put all my worldly pleasures aside.
He held out His hand, again and again
He offered me a home in the promised land.
I ran away time after time,
But no matter how hard I tried,
My life was unstable like shifting sand.
I finally realized "there's something about this man."

This man called Jesus,
The great I Am,
This man called Jesus,
There's something about this man.

Then one day, the Holy Spirit came in
And I asked Jesus to forgive my sin.
He took my old life and cast it in the sea
Then He started to make a new man out of me.
When I surrendered and gave Him control,
He gave me an eternal soul.
If I can be saved anybody can.
You better wake up and know there's something
about this man.

This man called Jesus,
The great I Am,
This man called Jesus,
There's something about this man.

2 Timothy 1:8; Revelation 6:9; 1 John, 5:11;
John 3:11; 4:39; 19:35; Luke 21:13.

⊰ 47 ⊱

SAY WHAT YOU MEAN

M y granddaughter Ellison Faith, or Ellie as we called her, was chasing my pet ducks all over the yard with a piece of bread in her hand. I had told her that if she walked up to them gently with a piece of bread that she could probably catch one. Ellie didn't know the meaning of the word *gently* and she was running around behind the ducks throwing bread at them. We all had a good laugh. My mind went back to a day when I was a little boy. I was at Grandma and Granddaddy's house. We were outside and there were little birds all over the yard. Grandma went inside and got a saltshaker filled with salt. She told me that if I would put salt on the birds' tails, I would be able to catch them. So off I went with the saltshaker, running around after the birds all over the place. Of course, they all flew off as I approached them. After a while, I disappointedly walked back to the porch. Grandma and Granddaddy were beside themselves laughing and I was mad. I took what they had said to heart. Of course, they told the truth. If I could put salt on the birds' tails, I surely could have caught them. Both these examples were innocent deceptions. There was no real harm in them.

On another occasion, Ellie was spending the day with me. She was about two years old. When it came to lunch time, I told her that I would cook her a peanut butter and jelly sandwich. She said "okay" and I commenced to making her a peanut butter and jelly sandwich. She got out her little table and chair and got ready to eat. When I took the peanut butter and jelly sandwich to her, she said, "but, Papa, you didn't cook it yet." She wasn't about to eat that sandwich until I cooked it. I had to take it back and stick it in the microwave for a few seconds before she would eat it. She took what I had said as being the literal truth and she made me stick to it.

My daddy used to tell me, when I was a kid, that he would be back in a few minutes. When I'd ask him where he was going, he would say, "going to see Annie Belle Clayton." Of course, I found out when I got older that he meant he was going to the ABC package store. I was just an old country boy and I didn't know what an ABC store was. Well one day, I asked my Mama if Annie Belle was any kin to us. She said, "Annie Belle who?" Then I said, "Annie Belle Clayton." She said, "I don't know her." "Why are you asking that?" Then I said, "well Daddy goes to see her every week." Mama didn't know what Annie Belle Clayton meant either. My daddy had some explaining to do when he got home. Thank God that one day, in 1976, my daddy decided

that he wasn't going to see Annie Belle Clayton anymore. If fact, we buried Annie Belle and my life was
changed forever. Daddy never drank another drop the
rest of his life. But that's a different story. The point
here is that Daddy didn't say exactly what he meant.
In a sense, he was deceiving me because he didn't want
me to know he was going to the liquor store. It almost
got him in trouble.

All of these things were innocent enough and didn't
cause any major trouble but in grown-up life, especially in our Christian walk, we need to say what we
mean. When we are witnessing to people, we need to
tell the truth. Too many Christians paint a rosy Utopia
when describing what it's like to be a Christian. Some
evangelists who teach prosperity gospel are deceiving
people and they will be held accountable for it. Any of
us who cause someone to stumble because of a lying,
deceptive tongue, will be held accountable. We live
in a day and time when false teachers are abundant.
Many will be led astray because of this. We must be
on guard against these false prophets who are teaching
and preaching what is not in God's Word. Be like my
granddaughter Ellie: demand the truth and hold one
another accountable.

> 2 Peter 2:1–22; Matthew 24:1–51; I John 4:1;
> Deuteronomy 13:1–18; Revelation 22:18;
> I Peter 1:20; 2 Timothy 4:3–4.

48

WELCOME TO 2020

I was sitting in the deer stand. It was the third day of muzzleloader season and the rut was in full swing in my part of the world. It should have been a morning filled with deer sightings, bucks chasing does, squirrels and birds feeding, and all other sorts of creatures stirring around. But this particular morning was eerie. Nothing was moving. The birds didn't come alive at first light with their singing. The turkeys didn't cackle as they flew down. It was like no morning I had ever seen. Perhaps, they sensed what was going on all over America.

It was the year 2020, a year that probably everyone in our nation would like to forget. It was an election year surrounded by riots, looting, deception, lies, and hate. Never had I heard of so much hate. There was racial tension, political uprising, and to top it all off, our nation was in the midst of a pandemic known as the Corona virus or COVID-19. It looked like aliens had landed all over the world. Some people were wearing masks everywhere they went, and some refused to wear them. People were quarantined. Churches cancelled their services for the most part. Church for most, was now online or sitting out in a parking lot listening to the service through a speaker. It was quite simply a time of absolute and total chaos.

So much can be said about 2020 that is negative, but I choose and tried to choose positive throughout that entire year. In spite of all the ugliness, pain, and suffering, God used that crazy year for good. I was a witness as five people came to salvation in Jesus—some in my own family—during a time when we were told we shouldn't go to church by our governor. I saw families start being families again because they were forced to be together. I watched kids learn about real life because they had to be home schooled. I heard more laughter from kids because they were outside experiencing God's creation more. I smiled when I heard people say things such as "I really want to hug someone" or "I miss seeing you" because the realization that we had been taking those things for granted was coming to light. I longed for love more than ever because I had witnessed so much hate. My foundation in King Jesus got stronger because earthly kings had failed me. My heart was stronger because it had been broken and ruptured so many times. My mirror was cleaner because I had to wipe all the self-worship away every time I looked into it. I saw people step up because they had been stepped on. I marveled at those who were on their knees more because they didn't have the strength to stand up any longer.

We always have the choice to die in the negative or live in the positive. One thing I know for sure: God used all of 2020 for good in some way. I choose to live in that knowledge. As 2021 was approaching, I was weary of the old year and excited for the new year, stronger, wiser, more hopeful, and ready to love. I know that the chapters are sometimes hard to bear, but thank God I know how the book ends. God gave me the lyrics to the song "Get Behind Me" one night when it seemed that it was hard to see anything good in what was going on in the world.

Get Behind Me

Walking down this road called life
We have to deal with heartache, trouble, and strife
And there's this thing that we call temptation.
We need to recognize that it's coming from satan
And say "get behind me," "get behind me."

All these feelings of hate and anger
Are put inside us by this worldly stranger.
Don't be confused, he's after you
But there's a way to stay out of danger,
Get behind me, get behind me.

Satan's lurking and he's trying to destroy.
If you call on Jesus, he can't take away your joy
Get behind me, get behind me.

If satan's knocking on your door this hour,
With salvation, you've got the power
To send him packing on his way
All you've got to do is say
"Get behind me," "get behind me."

Satan's lurking and he's trying to destroy.
If you call on Jesus, he can't take away your joy
Get behind me, get behind me.

Romans 8:28; Genesis 50:20; Proverbs 16:4;
Ecclesiastes 7:14; Matthew 16:23.

49

FACE YOUR FEAR

Three of my granddaughters, Emmie, Ellie, and Alyvia should be the poster children for No Fear. Alayna, is like me and a little more reserved; not really afraid of things but will check out the situation before diving in head first. Ellie is like a bull in a china shop. Sometimes she falls or runs into something and I just shake my head. I would be in traction, but she jumps up, laughs it off and takes off again. She reminds me of something that my daddy used to say. He would say "she is as tough as pig iron." Alyvia is what her Mama, Amanda, calls her wild child. She loves to chase down chickens and roosters so she can rub them. She is wide open from the time she hits the floor early in the morning until she says her prayers at bedtime. Alayna, watches her sister Alyvia in disbelief sometimes, then she will scope things out and usually join in the fun. Out of all of them, I would say that Emmie (Emmerson Grace), is the most reckless. From riding dirt bikes to jumping out of swings when she's ten feet in the air, she has no reservations about trying any potentially dangerous activity. Emmie lives life to the absolute fullest. She gets all that can be had out of every day and every activity.

I sometimes wish that I was more like my No Fear girls. I know that I've missed out on a lot in life because of my reservations. I'm not really afraid of very much, but many times while I'm evaluating things, I could be enjoying life a little more. There are a couple of things however that scare me to death. One is yellow jackets. I've been attacked so many times by them that I live in fear of them whenever I'm bush hogging with my tractor, weed eating, or mowing. You won't catch me in the woods after turkey season each year until the first frost arrives. It's not because of snakes but those terrifying yellow jackets. My wife says that I'm afraid of mice but I'm really not. I just don't like their beady little eyes and how they can show up anywhere. She does have to set the mouse traps and investigate if we hear a noise in the pantry though.

The second thing that I have a fear of, and this one is very serious in nature, is being rejected. This one has caused me to say "no" to God on occasion when He has asked me to do something with my talents and gifts. The fear of rejection is the reason that the best songs are never heard and the best stories are never read. It's the most common fear that there is. Getting up in front of an audience to sing, even if you are a great singer, can bring on a fear so strong that some people actually get sick. I've been there. I'm in awe of my granddaughters who get up and sing quite often at church and don't seem to be nervous one bit. My son Shane could play his guitar in front of the whole world and not be nervous. I'm built differently. My fear of rejection has kept me from using my talents many times. God doesn't want me to have that kind of fear. I know that but I still battle it constantly. One of the greatest fears I've ever faced was the fear that this book that I'm currently writing would be rejected. The hardest thing I've ever done was write the very first word in the opening chapter. Perhaps, that's why I chose a very short chapter to be the first. I didn't breathe the entire time I was writing it. Satan has tried to stop me several times while writing this book. He has told me that it was too elementary and that no one was going to read it because they didn't care one bit about my life experiences and what God had supposedly revealed to me. I've fought this battle with every word that I've written. I've fought self-worship like I did when I did the million pushups. I've wondered, because of that, if God really did call me to write this book. I believe with all my heart that He did. When I was talking to my friend Traci about the book and told her about my fear of it being rejected, this is what she had to say to me: "The thing you have to remember is that you have been justified, completely forgiven, and made righteous. Through God's eyes you are righteous! You are the man that He has called for this assignment. If God has called you to this, He will get you through this. Your assignment is to be obedient to do what He has called you to do. Pray every morning, 'Lord, flow through me today. Give me Your words through Your Holy Spirit.' He will do just that. Then write down what you feel the Holy Spirit telling you. Put aside your worry and replace it with confidence. Your obedience will bless so many! And it doesn't matter what people think. You are doing this to please God. When it pleases Him, that's really all that matters. When you do something this big, you will have critics. Just don't let them be a stumbling block. He that is in you is bigger than he who is in the world. Thank you for the honor to pray alongside you! Love you, Brother."

God has much to say about fear and the fear of rejection. He has been with me and given me the courage I needed to write this book. He set me apart to accomplish this task. I don't know how it could be said any better than Traci said it. Her words and the encouragement that Johnsie has given me throughout the process have given me the strength to cast my fears aside and let God type the words through my hands.

> Isaiah 41:10; Psalm 118:6; Romans 8:31–32;
> Exodus 9:16; Colossians 3:23.

50

ANGER WON'T CONSUME ME

I t was the first day of bow season. I had pictures of some really nice bucks and had watched them grow their antlers all summer via trail camera. I was more than excited, and I climbed into the stand with high expectations. The food and minerals were there, the cover was there, and I had even dug a small water hole for the animals to drink out of while they were feeding. I saw something heading my way out of the corner of my eye and soon there was a cow standing in front of me, then another, then another. In all, five cows came in to feed on my corn, clover, and even lick the minerals. I had spoken to the owner of the cows several times about keeping them off my property. Poorly maintained fences were the culprit. I could feel my face getting red as anger welled up inside me. This surely would mess up my hunting that day. After a while, the cows left, and I thought that maybe I would still see something.

About an hour later, I saw two bucks jump up out of the cutover in front of me and run off. I thought to myself that a coyote must have spooked them. Then I saw two of one of my neighbor's dogs running all through the cutover. The cows had made me angry, but this infuriated me. I had spoken to the owner of the dogs and asked her to please keep the dogs off my property during hunting season. It's one thing if a hunting dog mistakenly gets on my property, but these were no hunting dogs. They were Russian Bear Hounds, the kind that rush all over the neighbor's property and bear down on a biscuit. I was absolutely furious. I was so upset that I was shaking. *First cows and now dogs.* My angry mind was telling me that there was no way that I was going to see anything on this hunt, and I was about to get down out of the tree stand.

Then I saw movement, so I stayed in the stand. I was shaking uncontrollably, not because of buck fever but because I was so angry. I had been thinking about what I was going to say to the owners of the cows and dogs and the more I thought about it, the angrier I became. I was completely consumed to the point that I had lost control. Then four of the biggest bucks I had ever seen came out of the thickest part of my property. They were grazing on briars and there were antlers everywhere. The biggest buck gave me a 40-yard opportunity, and I drew my bow back and could hardly keep the pin sight on the deer much less on a particular spot on the deer. I was still shaking from anger, and I couldn't seem to calm down enough to settle the pin right behind the shoulder of the big buck. After what seemed like forever, but I'm sure was only a few seconds, I released my arrow and it sailed right over the buck's back. I had practiced that shot over and over, but my shaking had caused me to blow it. I had just missed the biggest buck I had ever seen. That didn't help my anger any at all.

I got down, found my bloodless arrow, and walked home. When I went into the house, Johnsie could tell that something was wrong. She's seen that dejected face too many times. She asked me what was wrong. I told her that I didn't want to talk about it right at that moment. A little while later, I shared the story with her and I was blaming the cows, the dogs, and the cow and dog owners. The truth of the matter is that it was all my fault for letting anger consume and control me. Those deer cared less about the cows and dogs than I did. They had become a natural part of the habitat.

After I had thought about it overnight, I realized what had happened. I knew that anger had been one of my biggest stumbling blocks my whole life and that I had to somehow get rid of it. I knew that I needed to pray about it and ask God to take it away. Anger is not always a bad thing. It's good for us to become angry about things that go on in our world—even Jesus became angry; however, when it controls us and consumes us, it is sin. I had let anger control me that day and it cost me a trophy buck. I asked God to forgive me and to help me get anger out of my life. I felt an immediate sense of peace and I knew that He was already working on it.

When I went to the deer stand the next afternoon, I had a much different perspective on things. I felt so peaceful and felt as if the whole world had been lifted off of my shoulders. I thanked God for giving me peace and just for the opportunity to be able to hunt this magnificent creature that He had created. I didn't see any deer that afternoon, but when I walked in the door, Johnsie didn't see any dejected looks, just a smile. She even said, "you must have gotten one." When I told her that I hadn't seen anything, she looked surprised to see that I was happy. I never saw any of those four bucks again, but three days later, I took the biggest buck of my life with my bow.

The Bible warns us that holding on to anger can lead to sin, so letting go of anger is what we need to be striving towards. Anger is an emotion like any other and we will have to deal with it. Letting go of it, I believe, can only be accomplished by letting God take it away. God says that anger lives in the fool's heart. He also says that it is foolish to hold grudges. Like so many other things, in order to be healthy and of God, anger has to be controlled. God has helped me deal with this by showing me that when I am angry, I should pray and when I'm upset, I should love. Focusing on the things of God and looking to Him as the ultimate example, I am able to conquer anger.

Psalm 37:8; Proverbs 14:17; 29:22; Ecclesiastes 7:9; Ephesians 4:26; Matthew 5:22.

51

OTHER REVELATIONS

God has given me so many revelations. Sometimes they don't relate to the outdoors, but almost always, the revelations come to me while I am spending time in God's great creation. Whether I'm hunting, fishing, hiking, sitting by a campfire, shark tooth or artifact hunting, or just taking in the fresh air and sunshine, God is constantly giving me words, stories, and sayings. I don't think He gives them to me to keep to myself, so I'm going to share some of those that didn't make it into another chapter.

Here are thoughts that God has given me while spending time in His creation:

> Salvation should be a "one time" occur-
> rence. A true salvation experience doesn't
> have to occur in your life over and over. As
> a matter of fact, if your experience was
> real, you won't feel the need to duplicate.
> On the other hand, repentance must be a

daily occurrence, or more often if needed. So, every time you fall short, ask for forgiveness, make a change, then move on.

The gift has already been given. No one can take it away.

Prayer is a huge tool when it comes to being fit. I'm fitna pray right now.

There are thousands and thousands of ways to die, but only one way to live.

True brokenness can't be repaired. It must be replaced with a new heart.

In order to truly be fed, we must first be hungry. Secondly, we must be willing to come to the table.

Don't gather to pray for rain if you are not going to bring an umbrella.

Sins of omission are sin, just like sins of commission.

As a fisherman, I understand that 90% of the fish will be in 10% of the water. As a Christian, I see that 90% of the work in the church is carried out by 10% of the congregation. I just don't understand that.

Christians, you better tell your children what's right and wrong according to God, or the world will give them its version.

In my personal walk, I have found that any day that passes that I don't shed a tear of humility or a tear of joy, is a day that I have lost focus. Some days require a single tear and some days require a rain storm.

Where the requirement is much, yet the sacrifice little; eventually the requirement may be removed along with the blessing.

How can the circle be unbroken if we aren't willing to hold the hand of the person on both sides of us?

If we are who we profess to be, we should desire goodly and godly for every soul, not just those in our circle.

We sometimes use up so much energy trying to receive forgiveness for the sins that Jesus has already cast into the sea, that we are too weary to be about the work that He has given us to do today.

For it to be perfect, it surely has to be that I love them only because He first loved me.

When we give to someone, to a cause or to the church, the perfection lies only in the sacrifice. No sacrifice, no giving.

In this day and time, we spend too much time debating right and wrong. It's truly not debatable. It has already been decided by God.

A flapping jaw is like a rusty old door hinge, it makes a lot of noise but usually locks up when speaking is appropriate.

It doesn't matter to me anymore whether my glass is half full or half empty because my cup surely runneth over.

The pulpit needs less feet ticklers and more toe crushers. I'm so thankful that I go to a church where steel toe shoes should be standard attire.

What is driving you today? Is it food, music, work, money, a hobby, another person? Make no mistake about it: Jesus is the only driver who will take you home.

His abundance and timing are so unbelievably unbelievable, that we must be believers to grasp it.

There is zero value in inhaling Jesus through your nostrils and exhaling satan from your mouth.

When we reach a point where sin has to come to a vote, we have a much bigger issue than whatever is being voted on.

We can't expect to make a difference if we aren't willing to be different.

I believe that every soul is so important to God that He may have created me or you for the sole purpose of winning one to Him.

I don't like it when people are labeled as recovering addicts and such. Make no mistake about it, we all are recovering from something. I'm so thankful that I have been recovered by the blood of Jesus.

"How dare anyone think they know more about where money should go than God does." —Rev. Walter Gentry, deceased.

Everyone seems to feel the need to jump on the bandwagon of proving they're not racist with long social media posts or kneeling to things other than God. If you aren't one, your life should speak for itself.

When your battle is against flesh, no man will back you up. When your battle is against satan, still no man will back you up. But God will.

I don't weigh in, in any way because whenever you weigh in, the way you weigh will be in-weighed in a way that you never intended. Some of you should adopt this policy.

Don't give up on this great nation until your knees have blisters on them.

We need to be less concerned about how or why people have landed where they are and more concerned with helping them take off again.

For me to love you, there is no requirement that I know you. For me to love you, there is a requirement that I know Jesus.

Trying to figure out all the variables in hunting, such as wind direction, barometric pressure, phase of the rut, phase of the moon, or whether or not a front is coming in gives me a headache. So, I just decided I'm going to hunt. The same applies to trying to figure God out. That gives me a headache too; so, I'm just going to trust and serve Him.

The answer isn't in a vaccine or a mask, an elephant, or a jackass. The answer isn't in a book or training, or all this complaining. The answer isn't in a song portraying what is wrong or a post fueling hate, three pages long. The answer is in the Holy Name of Jesus.

Daniel 2:19; Job 12:22; Jeremiah 33:3; Ephesians 3:3.

52

DEALING WITH CHRISTMAS

Christmas is a magical time of year. It's a time that seems to make us old folks feel like kids again. For me, it has gone from being excited about what I was going to get for gifts to being excited about giving to my children and grandchildren. Johnsie and I always try to give to others, especially during this season. Christmas really should be about giving and receiving. It should be about the gift that God gave us in His son, Jesus, and about receiving the gift of eternal life.

With that being said, I've heard the Christmas story many times over my life. Up until this year however, it has always spoken to me in the same ways. This year, God revealed a couple of things to me that I had never thought about before. First, He showed me something through Mary that I had never grasped before. When Mary was told by Gabriel that she was highly favored and would bring forth a son whose name would be Jesus, she was troubled, not for the reasons that you might think. She wasn't troubled because this was going to bring her heartache and shame in this world. She wasn't troubled because she had this high calling, and it was going to be uncomfortable and would cost her much. She was troubled because she didn't feel worthy of this high calling, of this kind of grace. It got me to thinking about the callings that God has placed on my life and whether I was troubled because I didn't feel worthy or because it was going to be uncomfortable and cost me something. I prayed this prayer: "Father, help me to be troubled like Mary when You call me to something that I'm surely not worthy of and not capable of. Help me to have faith like Mary's and not be concerned about what the calling will cost me but how it will glorify You. Amen."

The other thing that God revealed to me came just after Christmas and God used my granddaughter Alyvia as the instrument to speak to me. I knew that Amanda, Alayna, and Alyvia were taking down their Christmas decorations. It was a week or so after Christmas. I called their house and Alyvia answered. I asked her if they had gotten everything straightened out from Christmas and she said, "no we're still dealing with it." First, I thought that was hilarious coming from a five-year-old. Then it really got me to thinking about all the things that people were dealing with. I was burdened by the fact that many people had not dealt with Christmas. Many people had not dealt with the birth of The King. I prayed for those who had not taken the opportunity to deal with the Savior who was born humbly and died cruelly just so that we could live.

The Christmas story will always look different to me from now on. I don't know how many Christmases I have left, but I'm surely going to make every single one count. I'm going to give, celebrate what I have received, pray for those who have not dealt with it, and be filled with joy.

Isaiah 9:6; Luke 1:26–38.

CPSIA information can be obtained
at www.ICGtesting.com
Printed in the USA
BVHW040755260821
615304BV00007B/37

9 781662 815317